THE
Leadership
Difference

by Robert E. Logan
with Tara Miller

 COPYRIGHT

Published by Logan LeadershipVisit us at http://loganleadership.com

ISBN 10: 1-944955-40-2

ISBN 13: 978-1-944955-40-3

Printed in the United States of America 2017- First Edition

24 23 22 21 20 19 18 17   10 9 8 7 6 5 4 3 2 1

CONTENTS

Foreword by Colin Noyes   1

Introduction: My Moses Problem   3

1. The Foundation: Most of Your Leadership Problems Are Actually Discipleship Problems   15

2. Your Own Personal Development Don't Skip This Chapter   31

3. Who Do You Need? Getting the Right Players on Your Team   53

4. Developing People: Creating a Framework for Growth   69

5. Team-building, Part 1: Building One Another Up   81

6. Team-building, Part 2: Spurring One Another On   95

7. Discernment and Focus: Getting a Sense of Direction   111

8. Leading Change: Herding Cats and Other Feats of Patience   127

9. Communication Skills: It Takes Three Cuts to Get It Right   149

10. Advanced People Development: Working with Key Leaders   169

11. Organizational Development: Shifting Gears to Avoid Stalling Out   191

12. Financial and Legal Practicalities: Staying Out of Jail   209

13. Empowering and Releasing Others: Giving It All Away   223

Appendices

    A: Dimensions of Discipleship   237

    B: Leadership Skills   241

    About the Author   245

    About Logan Leadership   245

    Love God | Love Others | Make Disciples   247

    Discipleship Resources   249

    Leadership Resources   251

    Training Opportunities   252

Acknowledgments   253

 FOREWORD

by Colin Noyes

A few years ago, the phone rang in my office. It was a young leader who asked me if I would coach him. As is usual for me, I asked him some questions about where he thought God was taking him in the future. He proceeded to tell me that he had listened to and read everything that had been produced by the leader of a certain megachurch in the States, and that God was calling him to be the leader of a megachurch as well.

I asked him some of the same questions that Bob Logan has raised in the book you are about to read. His answers showed that he had a lot of work to do to lead his current church effectively, and that the megachurch vision was a long way off. He decided I wasn't the coach for him and went looking for someone else who could help him.

No matter where God might be taking you in the future: If you have a leadership role, then you should read this practical down-to-earth book, to make sure that your foundations for the future are anchored on solid rock and not moving sand.

I first met Bob Logan thirty years ago, in a seminar he was leading on church planting, and we have stayed connected since. He has been a major contributor to my development as a Christian leader, and we have worked together on a number of projects over the years.

Bob has been a successful church planter in a church that planted churches, a mission strategist who has worked with National

Leaders in more than thirty countries around the world, a resource developer who has given the church worldwide materials on church planting, church health, coaching, and leadership, and has authored and coauthored numerous books on leadership, planting and multiplication, discipleship and coaching.

This current book by Bob provides important practical, foundational teaching for Christian leaders.

Enjoy!

INTRODUCTION
My Moses Problem

The first time I was planting a church, I found that I was getting tired and discouraged every two weeks. Some planters have a weekly cycle and some a monthly schedule, but mine seemed to be a lunar cycle. For whatever reason, I'd start feeling really down every two weeks. I prayed the psalms, crying out to God, asking for his help, praying for perspective. I was on the lookout for unconfessed sin. I tried counting my blessings and practicing gratitude. Normally these approaches would help me regain my equilibrium, and for a while they did. But after a year or so, things were worse. Nothing seemed to help when I was feeling discouraged.

Then the thought came, "Why don't you sit down and draw an org chart of the church?" My first response was one of irritation. "An org chart? Hmm... well, since God isn't answering my prayers, I might as well do that."

I wrote my name down at the top, drew the chart, and discovered that I had twenty-seven direct reports. That's twenty-seven lines going to my name with arrows. I threw my pen down on the paper and thought, "No wonder I'm tired! I don't have a spiritual problem here. I have a Moses problem. I'm trying to do too much stuff myself."

Consider Moses—burning himself out in ministry due to his leadership style—before his father-in-law came in with some helpful advice for a different approach:

> The next day Moses took his seat to serve as judge for the people, and they stood around him from morning till evening.

When his father-in-law saw all that Moses was doing for the people, he said, "What is this you are doing for the people? Why do you alone sit as judge, while all these people stand around you from morning till evening?"

Moses answered him, "Because the people come to me to seek God's will. Whenever they have a dispute, it is brought to me, and I decide between the parties and inform them of God's decrees and instructions."

Moses' father-in-law replied, "What you are doing is not good. You and these people who come to you will only wear yourselves out. The work is too heavy for you; you cannot handle it alone. Listen now to me and I will give you some advice, and may God be with you. You must be the people's representative before God and bring their disputes to him. Teach them his decrees and instructions, and show them the way they are to live and how they are to behave. But select capable men from all the people—men who fear God, trustworthy men who hate dishonest gain—and appoint them as officials over thousands, hundreds, fifties and tens. Have them serve as judges for the people at all times, but have them bring every difficult case to you; the simple cases they can decide themselves. That will make your load lighter, because they will share it with you. If you do this and God so commands, you will be able to stand the strain, and all these people will go home satisfied."

Moses listened to his father-in-law and did everything he said (Exod. 18:13–24).

What did I learn? That spiritual problems need to be addressed with spiritual tools. Leadership problems—although absolutely requiring a strong spiritual foundation—need to be addressed with leadership tools. And I had a leadership problem.

Notes from Colin:

Periodically throughout this book you'll see boxes with some commentary from Colin Noyes. We go back years working on many projects together, and I appreciate his international perspective. He works with ministry leaders and churches in Australia and the South Pacific. Because I value Colin's input, I've invited him to write in the margins here for the benefit of readers. And an as Australian, he does use international English spellings.

I'm not the first or last person to identify the fact that I had a leadership problem. The ministry workload Moses believed he had to carry was not only wearing him out but was wearing out the people. Recognizing the problem and changing not only allowed him to survive, but enabled the people to live in peace (good outcome).

> **Spiritual problems need to be addressed with spiritual tools. Leadership problems need to be addressed with leadership tools.**

In Acts 6:1–7 the disciples of Jesus also faced a leadership problem, which they solved by bringing others onto the team. This allowed the word of God to keep spreading, the number of disciples in Jerusalem to increase greatly, and a large number of priests to begin obeying the faith (great outcome). Many of those in ministry confuse calling and praxis, and in so doing perpetuate serious problems for themselves and others.

Over the next few years, largely by trial and error, I succeeded in planting a new church. As it grew *and* as I faced questions about leading an organization and managing a staff, I found myself unprepared for many of the challenges. Sometimes I needed to wear the hat of a shepherd, sometimes the hat of a preacher, and sometimes the hat of a leader and manager.

Since planting a church, I've pastored, coached pastors and planters, consulted with denominations, and created resources to help with church leadership. Over time I've found that probably sixty percent of what a pastor does falls into the category of leading and managing. Even in parachurch ministries or other nonprofits, the number usually hovers around fifty percent.

Have you ever felt like you weren't fully equipped for your leadership role? Like you needed a bit more practical guidance in the "what-to-dos" of ministry? Like the barriers you're running up against aren't specifically theological, but are more about how to lead people and get along with them as you work together?

If so, this book is written for you. It focuses specifically on leadership skills for ministry leaders. That certainly includes pastors and staff members at local churches, but it also includes those in parachurch ministry or nontraditional missional ministry. A large portion of readers may also be lay leaders or bivocational leaders. Whatever your specific role is and whether or not you're getting paid, are beside the point. This book is written for people who have a heart for the ministry and are leading others in that pursuit.

Anyone in a position of ministry leadership, whether they're leading a church, a team, a small group, or the nation of Israel, needs skills and strategies like these—skills and strategies that result in lightening your own load, developing the skills of others, and sending all the people home satisfied. (Well, I suppose I can't guarantee that last one but it sure would be nice, wouldn't it?)

Not working harder—working differently

Many of the leadership and management skills covered in this book are ones I learned along the way in my own ministry roles— largely by running into barriers and questions. How do I delegate? How do I reorganize as the ministry grows? How do I develop people but also get the work done that needs to be done? In most cases, these are not the skills taught in seminary—yet they're critical in leading any type of ministry. Essentially, this is the book I wish I had forty years ago when I was in seminary.

Unfortunately, most ministry leaders who weren't trained in leadership or management skills simply take the approach of just trying harder. Have you ever found yourself in those shoes? When faced with the problems of organizing a growing ministry, do you feel overwhelmed? Are you not

> This is the book I wish I had forty years ago when I was in seminary.

getting the results you want? Do you find yourself just working harder or longer at what you're already doing?

> **A note from Colin**
>
> *If you find yourself working harder and harder have you ever stopped to ask why? This book will offer you some excellent insights and skills development as a leader, but it won't help you if your problem is a "need to be needed," a "separation of clergy and laity" view of ministry, or an "I'm paid to do the ministry" problem. Like all behaviour, it is wise to ask what is underlying what you do. You may need to do some serious corrective work first.*

It won't work. I know—I've tried it. Working harder will just increase the feelings of overload and frustration. It's like trying to bail out a leaky boat instead of going underneath to fix the hole. This book is not about working harder, but working differently. It's about fixing the leaks so you can continue growing and expanding your ministry more wisely and effectively—without losing your mind or your health.

If you are in a position of ministry leadership, and you desire to lead well and effectively while both developing others *and* getting the job done, this book was written with you in mind. Think of it as a way of listening to your father-in-law, who has gone before you and learned some things the hard way: "Let the wise listen and add to their learning, and let the discerning get guidance" (Prov. 1:5).

The God connection

Leadership and management skills are not just an add-on to ministry leadership. They are integral to the work of the ministry and go hand-in-hand with the spiritual element. If you want to have a great small group ministry, a great compassion ministry, a great new church, you need to stop and recognize what God is doing, and discern how he is calling you to be a part of it.

Then—given that God is already at work—your job as a leader is to help shape the results of his Spirit at work. How can you organize what God is already doing, in order to achieve maximum fruitfulness? The fruit is growing on the branches. Will you harvest and preserve it, or let it rot? Will you continue to prune the branches and plant new trees, or will you let the seeds go to waste?

That was the critical difference between the Welsh revival and the Wesley revival. In both cases, the church saw a movement of the Holy Spirit resulting in many conversions. The Holy Spirit was clearly at work. The leaders of the Welsh revival refused to organize the results of that work because they thought it was unspiritual to do so. That revival had a great start, but petered out. John Wesley did choose to organize, and had a hundred-year run with fruit lasting into today. He organized the results of what God was doing to get the maximum yield that he could for the church. It was the leadership that effectively determined whether a movement would develop or not.

A note from Colin:

John Wesley was asked by his contemporaries why he could not be content with just preaching, and letting God take care of the converts without his method of discipleship. He replied, "Every time I have tried that, most fell by the wayside. Whether it is one-on-one or class training, discipleship is God's plan for His church."

George Whitfield, a contemporary of Wesley, said "the difference between the lasting success of John Wesley's ministry and mine was discipleship and Wesley's class systems. My brother Wesley acted wisely—the souls that were awakened under his ministry he joined in classes, and thus preserved the fruits of his labour. I neglected to do this and my converts are a rope of sand." Wesley also said, "I am more and more convinced that the devil himself desires nothing more than this, that the people of any place should be half-awakened and then left to themselves to fall asleep again."

Competent leaders can maximize the fruit of what God is doing, while poor leadership can squander it. Leadership doesn't produce spiritual dynamics; only the Holy Spirit can do that. However, lack of effective leadership can diminish the *impact* of those spiritual dynamics.

Consider what that difference could look like in your own ministry. If you read this book and put the principles into practice, what will you get? After all, learning these skills and strategies takes effort, thought, and practice.

> **Good leadership leaves a lasting impact. It's what keeps people pressing on to the next culture, the next street, the next act of service, even in the face of difficulty or discouragement.**

It should yield something. The investment is big, but the payoff is also significant.

If you practice leadership well, you could effectively lead your organization toward the accomplishment of the mission. You could facilitate the holistic development of your people. You could structure your organization so it flourishes in the long-term. Good leadership leaves a lasting impact. It's what keeps people pressing on to the next culture, the next street, the next act of service, even in the face of difficulty or discouragement.

Do you want that for your people? Consider what could be accomplished. You could see your people working together effectively as they live on mission together. You could see them serving those in need in ways geared to doing the most good. You could see discipling relationships multiply from one person to another to another to another. You could see your organization grow—but grow responsibly, ensuring that all people are cared for. You could see your people communicating well with one another, and relating positively to those who are different from themselves. You could see ministries working in concert rather than competing with one another. You could see people growing in their giftedness, being stretched and challenged to try new things to serve and grow. You could see networks of supportive relationships that allow people to fully experience the life and mission God has for them.

You could see people flourishing. When the Holy Spirit is at work, you'll be ready and prepared to harvest the fruit.

If you are feeling like I did when I discovered my Moses problem—overwhelmed in ministry and uncertain how to get it all done—there is hope. This book is designed to help you expand your leadership capacity, and to do so wisely. You've likely already been trying really hard, but maybe you're not getting the results you're looking for. You know you could be making more progress, getting more results. If your vision outstrips your capacity, redoubling your efforts won't work—it will just burn you out.

Instead of trying harder, try it differently. That's what the rest of this book is about.

Why I'm writing

I have three basic purposes as I write this book.

The first is to make the critical connection between discipleship and leadership. My last book was called *The Discipleship Difference*, and this one is called *The Leadership Difference*. That's not a coincidence. This book is a sequel—a part two. Discipleship is the essential foundation of all Christian leadership. We may have great leadership skills, but without discipleship, we're nothing more than resounding gongs or clanging cymbals (1 Cor. 13:1). We need both: deep personal discipleship first, and then strong leadership skills built on that solid foundation.

My second purpose is rather straightforward: to introduce and unpack essential leadership skills needed to be effective in ministry. I don't mean "effective" in the business or worldly sense of the term, but effective in terms of living out God's calling for you as well as you can. Understanding and utilizing good leadership skills make a difference in how well we can do what God has called

> Good leadership skills make a difference in how well we can do what God has called us to do. Good intentions aren't enough.

us to do. Good intentions aren't enough. I've seen plenty of well-meaning leaders flounder on the sharp rocks of ministry. We can learn a great deal of practical skills and strategies from those who have gone before us, whether that's Moses or the pastor who mentored us. Let's use all the resources God has put at our disposal. Accomplishing his mission is worth it.

The third purpose, not to be overlooked, is learning how to pass these leadership skills along to others. Part of being a good leader is not just the ability to do things yourself, but developing these same skills in others. Not one of us is indispensable. We are all here just for a time, a season. As Moses wrote in Psalm 90:5–6, 10:

> *Yet you sweep people away in the sleep of death—*
> *they are like the new grass of the morning:*
> *In the morning it springs up new,*
> *but by evening it is dry and withered.*
>
> *Our days may come to seventy years,*
> *or eighty, if our strength endures;*
> *yet the best of them are but trouble and sorrow,*
> *for they quickly pass, and we fly away.*

Therefore, we must pass these skills on to others—especially the next generation, who will be leading long after we ourselves are gone. Eventually, we will be part of that group of leaders who have gone before and can pass what we have learned to others.

A note from Colin:

Too many current leaders measure their influence by the number of followers they have. According to Tom Peters, "Leaders don't create followers... they create more leaders." If you want to have a church that is enduring, having good leaders is not enough. We must build a culture of leadership throughout our church or movement that continually cultivates more leaders. This principle was established by Jesus, and followed by Paul in his ministry (2 Tim. 2:2).

What I'm assuming

Before we begin, I should also clarify a few assumptions I am working on.

One is that I believe leadership skills can be learned. There is certainly a spiritual gift of leadership, and the skills in this book will come more easily to some than to others. But with help and hard work, there are some basic skills everyone can learn, regardless of personality or gifting.

Another assumption is that leadership and management are connected. I do see a distinction between leadership and management. Leadership is more a matter of visioning, setting direction, and motivating people to embrace the way forward. The Greek word used in Romans 12 that is most often translated "leader" means "presides before." Management (sometimes called administration) is more a matter of figuring out the strategy of how to get there. The word used in 1 Corinthians 12 is "navigator of a ship." The destination is already a given, but the captain must steer around rocks to get there.

The leadership we're talking about in this book includes both elements: leadership and management. The church needs both and the two gifts intersect and overlap. A good leader cannot divorce herself from management, and a good manager cannot manage effectively without some type of leadership in place to provide direction.

A third assumption is one you'll see in the very structure of this book: Various leadership skills are all interconnected. They are not practiced in isolation from one another, but are orchestrated together to achieve the desired end. Consider the example of a surgeon: She must know how to use each of her instruments and for what purpose. She must be able to perform certain basic techniques, such as making an incision and suturing a wound. But she also needs to be able to see the big picture: how to apply the right tool at the right time for the right purpose and in the right order. The skills must be integrated together correctly.

As a result, you'll see many cross-references throughout this book. By necessity a book is written in a linear fashion; I had to choose what topics to address in what order. Yet leadership is not linear, so you'll see me referring to other sections throughout the book where you can find related material. Sometimes I'll introduce a seed thought that will be unpacked more later. Sometimes I'll refer back to a previous chapter.

Due to that structure, this book is one you'll want to work through more than once because of the extensive interconnectedness of the leadership competencies. Even better, work through it with a few other leaders. Not only is the support invaluable, but you can learn so much from one another as you journey together. My prayer as you read this is that you'll be able to work together with others toward maximizing the fruitfulness of all that God is doing... and he is able to do much more than we ask or imagine.

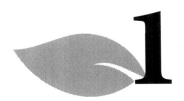

THE FOUNDATION

Most of Your Leadership Problems Are Actually Discipleship Problems

A few years back a colleague of mine was consulting with a group of pastors and other Christian leaders. The topic at hand was leadership. He asked the group to name some of the challenges they were facing with leadership development in their ministries.

The group had no difficulty coming up with various problems: lack of commitment, irregular attendance, current leaders being too busy, inability to communicate effectively, moral failings in leaders, conflicts between people with opposing agendas, and on and on and on. They filled that whiteboard.

When the venting and frustration had subsided, my colleague asked the group, "Looking at the board, how many of these leadership problems are actually discipleship problems?" Silence. The realization sunk in that many of what we consider leadership issues are actually discipleship issues.

When he told me this story, I was curious. I decided to test the theory myself. I've since repeated the exercise numerous times and have found that between seventy and eighty percent of the practical problems people identify are attributable to discipleship issues. We have people in leadership positions who are not growing, committed disciples themselves.

> ### A note from Colin:
>
> If you are working through this book with others, try the following exercise: Draw a line down the middle of a whiteboard and ask people to identify the characteristics of a disciple on the left-hand side. When they are finished, ask them to list the distinct characteristics of a leader on the right-hand side—only those characteristics that aren't already mentioned under the "disciple" heading. Most of the time there is nothing on the right-hand side. You and your group will discover that almost all of the qualities of an effective leader are founded on the fact that he or she is primarily a wholehearted disciple of Jesus.

What's the solution? We need to develop leaders only from those people who are already growing disciples—and we need to help people in existing positions of leadership get on the discipleship track if they're not already. Leaders need to be firmly rooted in an authentic, personal relationship with God as they grow in following him. That's qualification number one. Without that in place nothing else holds, no matter how skilled or intelligent or inspiring a person may be.

> Since then, no prophet has risen in Israel like Moses, whom the Lord knew face to face (Deut. 34:10).

Although this book is not primarily about discipleship, it does begin with it because discipleship is the necessary foundation upon which everything else rests.

Topics we'll cover in this chapter include:

- The connection between leadership and discipleship
- Discipleship competencies
- Infusing discipleship into our process
- Leadership competencies
- Sensitivity to the Holy Spirit
- A vision for integration of discipleship and leadership

The connection between leadership and discipleship

Consider Jesus' image of building a house on a solid foundation:

> "Why do you call me, 'Lord, Lord,' and do not do what I say? As for everyone who comes to me and hears my words and puts them into practice, I will show you what they are like. They are like a man building a house, who dug down deep and laid the foundation on rock. When a flood came, the torrent struck that house but could not shake it, because it was well built. But the one who hears my words and does not put them into practice is like a man who built a house on the ground without a foundation. The moment the torrent struck that house, it collapsed and its destruction was complete" (Luke 6:46–49).

Now consider someone who desires to become a Christian leader. He may have solid theological knowledge and know how to communicate it in a compelling way. He may have good interpersonal skills and provide sound counsel to resolve conflicts between people. He may have strong leadership skills and know how to get people on board with his agenda and direction. He may be able to put the right people in the right places and grow the organization.

Those are all good things. They're essential skills for Christian leaders and we'll address many of them later in this book. Yet if those skills are built directly on the ground, without digging down and laying a solid foundation of personal discipleship and character, what will happen? Those fancy walls, with all their craftsmanship and beauty, will come crashing down when the ground shifts or the wind blows or the rain comes down. The work will have been a waste, and often the building will hurt people inside or nearby when it falls down. That's what happens when churches and ministries collapse due to character and discipleship issues in their leaders.

A note from Colin:

I enjoy watching a television series called "Air Crash Investigations." It is based on the research work of National Transportation Safety Boards, who try to work out what went wrong. What I have observed in almost all situations is that it is a train of events—not a single mistake, event, or problem—that brings down a plane.

Over the years I have been called on to work with leaders whose ministries have come crashing down. Each time, I have discovered a chain of events that led to the crash—a poor or nonexistent entry into the discipleship journey, moving people into leadership too quickly, interpreting charisma or business skills as Christian leadership, sending people to colleges for training knowing many of these places are disconnected from the front line of ministry, etc. It's not hard to work out what went wrong.

On the other hand, let's look at a different scenario. Say there's another person who wants to become a Christian leader. In this case, she spends time laying that foundation of personal discipleship, living in community with others even when it's hard, listening to the Holy Spirit, and acting in loving obedience to what she's hearing. From the outside, others can't see any real progress. Is she building something? They just see a lot of digging around in the dirt. But then one day they notice walls going up... again with fine craftsmanship and beauty. The electrical wiring is added and the roof goes on. The walls are covered with high-quality paint. It looks just as good as the first house did, but this house holds strong in the face of storms and wind and shifting ground. Her strong leadership skills were built on the solid foundation of discipleship.

That's the relationship of discipleship to leadership. The two work together holistically, and we need both to be effective Christian leaders. Discipleship is the often less visible but absolutely essential foundation upon which leadership must rest in order to be viable in the long term. Without it, everything else collapses.

> Discipleship is the often less visible but absolutely essential foundation upon which leadership must rest. Without it, everything else collapses.

Now keep in mind that there is a third option you may run across from time to time: the person who wants to be a Christian leader but assumes that the only necessary qualification for that role is discipleship. This person does not believe leadership skills are necessary in spiritual contexts, and prefers to function solely as a shepherd or a spiritual director. In this third scenario, the person has a tendency to overspiritualize things, discounting or minimizing the necessity of an organization. However, the church is designed as a body, and the body functions as each part does its work. Life itself depends on interconnection and connectedness. This perspective of hyperspiritualization is completely different from what we are addressing in this book, and if you are working with someone like this, you'll need to address assumptions about leadership skills being unspiritual before he or she will find anything else here helpful.

But for those that do believe that leadership skills are helpful and necessary within ministry contexts, discipleship is the foundation upon which leadership is built. What does this mean for how we approach the connection between discipleship and leadership in our ministries?

Often when we talk about leadership development, what we're really doing is going back and filling in discipleship pieces that were missed. Certainly that's needed, as pieces are missing with all of us. And certainly discipleship is a lifelong endeavor; we never finish and call the job done. But how much better to start with a good foundation of character and core life skills, and then add leadership—as well as ongoing discipleship—from there?

This is a book about leadership skills. But it *assumes* you're also a growing disciple. A growing disciple doesn't mean being perfect. None of us can pull that off, and none of the leaders in the Bible could either. Moses certainly didn't. He got mad at his people, lost his temper with God, and really didn't want to be in leadership in the first place. And this is someone described as one who "spoke to God face to face, as one speaks to a friend" (Exod. 33:11).

Being a growing disciple means being someone who is actively developing and transforming—trying, failing, learning, repenting, listening, trying again, being honest. Remember that being a disciple doesn't mean we've completed all of these areas and checked them off our list, but rather that we are beginning with a foundation of discipleship and continuing to grow in that.

Let's start with discipleship first. Once people are living and growing as disciples, we can begin work more effectively on leadership development.

Discipleship competencies

So what discipleship competencies should we ensure are in place as a foundation for leadership? What does a disciple actually look like? What does he or she actually do? I've addressed these competencies in my prior book, *The Discipleship Difference*. You can look there for a more thorough examination, but here are the basic categories that form the foundation:

Experiencing God: Intentionally and consistently engaging with God in such a way that you open yourself to a deeper understanding of him and deeper relationship with him (Luke 10:27).

Spiritual Responsiveness: Actively listening to the Holy Spirit and taking action according to what you are hearing (Prov. 3:5–6; Gal. 5:25; James 1:22).

Sacrificial Service: Doing good works even when it's costly, inconvenient or challenging (Gal 2:10; Eph. 2:10).

Generous Living: Faithfully stewarding what God has given you so you can contribute toward the advancement of the Kingdom (Matt. 25:14–15; Luke 16:10).

Disciplemaking: Living in obedience to the great commission given by Jesus, which entails making more and better followers of Christ (Matt. 28:19–20).

Personal Transformation: Changing your attitudes and behaviors in positive ways as a result of your relationship with God and others (Rom. 12:2).

Authentic Relationships: Engaging with other people in ways that reflect the heart of God toward them (Matt 7:12).

Community Transformation: Personal involvement with others to facilitate positive change where you live and beyond (Eph. 3:20–21; Rev. 21:5).

For more detail on these areas of discipleship, including how they are expressed in behaviors and how they can be measured and developed, please see the Appendix.

Imagine a person who was already growing and developing in each of these areas. How much more easily would you be able to help mold their leadership skills? Instead of splitting your attention—one day working on helping them vision-cast (a leadership competency) and the next day working on helping them make and keep their promises (a basic discipleship competency)—you could build on the foundation of a growing disciple. That doesn't mean you'll never have to address discipleship issues, of course, but it means you can already assume a basic commitment to the discipleship process. If people have already begun with discipleship, the segue to leadership is not so difficult.

Infusing discipleship into our context

Some of you may be thinking at this point, "That sounds good, but we don't really have a discipleship process in place. Plus, we already have leaders in place who probably don't have a thriving foundation of discipleship. What are we supposed to do in this situation?" If you keep doing what you've already been doing, you'll keep having the same problems you're having now. So here are a few strategies to consider.

Be sure to start something new. Most likely you really can't start something new with everyone all at once. But unless you start somewhere, you'll never get any traction. If you want to train small group leaders in a new way, begin doing so with the new leaders. Otherwise, you'll just be perpetuating the old way of doing things and they'll be indoctrinated into the old patterns.

Offer a two-track process. You could use one track when you're working with new people, and a second track when you're working with existing leaders, building discipleship in after the fact. On the first track, there's a clear process of discipleship, then they move into being developed as leaders. In this way, you can build in both from day one with new people. They know that if they're serving with you, they're growing in their faith. That's just part of the deal, and you're invested in helping them with both. For the second track, you could then work toward retrofitting existing leaders. One word of warning with this two-track process: Do your best to avoid an "us vs. them" mentality. When starting something new, there's a strong temptation to disparage the old. These are often the faithful people who have held the ministry together for years, so you need to find a way to respect their contribution, even as you lead them toward what's next.

A note from Colin:

The temptation is to start the first track and not share what you are doing. This is usually not a good idea. Let people know what you are doing but cradle it in the history of your group. Tell stories of change from the past and celebrate those changes. Show how God's people are to be on a constant adventure of growth until Jesus comes. Paul talked about "forgetting the past" and "straining toward the future." The purpose of storytelling is to create a new perspective on things so people can adapt their way of thinking. Keep up the momentum until the new idea is the "natural way of things."

Make incremental changes. Sometimes slow and steady is the best way to make changes. Say you have a church board meeting that is all business and no discipleship. How might you be able to introduce a more extended time of prayer or community-building? Possibly you could begin opening the meetings regularly by asking everyone, "How did you experience God this month?" Then consider: Who are a

> Sometimes slow and steady is the best way to make changes.

couple of people on the board that might be responsive to engaging in a discipling relationship with you? How could you set an example of integrating discipleship behaviors with your leadership? In ways like these you can sow seeds and incrementally introduce change.

Try a pilot project. Another helpful strategy is to create a voluntary pilot project. Gather just willing people to try a new approach to building discipleship into leadership. One church created a gathering of leaders from different ministry areas to work through Blackaby's book *Experiencing God*. If the pilot project is successful, it may catch on from there. Plus, then you're not trying to force those who are unwilling into a new strategy.

Provide coaching. I spend a lot of my time coaching people and groups about how to approach leadership development issues such as this one. Sometimes it's helpful to brainstorm and process about your specific ministry context with someone who's outside of it. Consider finding a coach or someone who can help you figure out an effective way to move forward.

These are some strategies for bringing discipleship into leadership. But what precisely do we mean by leadership? Just as we looked at competencies for discipleship, so we must look at competencies for leadership.

Leadership competencies

Every believer is called to be a disciple. But not every believer is called to be a leader. Therefore, all believers are called to grow in the essential discipleship competencies above. But for leaders, what *additional* competencies do they need for effective leadership? What leadership skills do we need to build on top of that foundation of discipleship?

A note from Colin:

Competencies are often used to cover a number of different terms. It is important to define these more specifically:

- **Skills** *are defined as the ability or capacity to do something that is acquired through specific training. If you want to be a good coach you need to develop two key skills: listening and asking questions.*

- **Traits** *are at the other end of the spectrum. They are often linked to a person's behaviour. Some people are introverts and others are extroverts.*

- **Competencies** *are behaviours we display in order to translate knowledge and skills, and to leverage the traits to perform in a role. A good leader takes what he has learned, expresses it in the context of who he is, and practices using different approaches to increase performance levels.*

Any competencies along these lines would answer the question, "What does a leader need to do?" Consider the daily and weekly life of some Christian leaders you respect. What do you see them doing? There may be some obviously pastoral things like preaching, doing hospital visits, or leading a group or Bible study, but look deeper. They are probably also developing and investing in newer leaders. They are probably engaging in ongoing growth or spiritual practices in their own lives.

Then of course, things come up. They may be dealing with interpersonal conflicts. They may be trying to get their ministry on course in a different direction. They may be overseeing other staff or volunteers. They may be planning and implementing new ministry initiatives. There are many possibilities, and the most effective leaders know how to do the right thing at the right time.

Over the last forty years of working with leaders, here are six key themes I've noticed. Each represents an area in which leaders need to be growing. What I have below isn't comprehensive, just an overview. You can find a more detailed unpacking of Christian leadership competencies in the appendix, along with references to resources designed for teaching and developing these competencies in others.

Personal Development includes essential skills that leaders use to govern their own personal lives such as time, money, and prioritization. These are the foundations on which we can build additional leadership skills.

Developing Leaders is an essential part of being a leader oneself. Unless we plan to do all the work by ourselves, we'll need to train new leaders right from the start in order to begin developing and investing in others. In this way, we can build reproduction into the DNA of our leadership development system.

Leading Teams can be one of the more challenging parts of leadership. It requires a diverse skill set, including coaching, supervision, delegation, facilitating meetings, and building community.

Organizational Development means being able to run an organization—and to do so as the organization continues to develop and grow over time. If a ministry is successful, it generally extends to include and serve more people. Skills in this area include casting vision, gaining buy-in, and creating long-term plans.

Communication Skills include effective listening, asking good questions, getting our point across, and dealing with resistance and challenges. All these skills look much easier to put into practice than they actually are, particularly when trying to communicate with people different from ourselves.

Pastoral Skills include certain practical skills needed by almost all leaders in one capacity or another (regardless of whether "pastor" is in their title): shepherding, mentoring, facilitating small group discussion, and public speaking.

If someone were to be trained in all of these skills—in increasing capacity—imagine what a strong leader that person would be. Yet no one's development is ever in a straight line or a neatly filled-out chart. People will come in with certain areas more developed than others. Their background, personality, and spiritual gifting will play into what they already have largely in place and what they need to intentionally develop. So even as we take strategic steps to train our leaders in these skills, we cannot underestimate the importance of being guided by the Spirit. That holds true in our own leadership development, as well as our focus in developing leadership skills in others.

Sensitivity to the Holy Spirit

Remember when you were first a believer, discovering and exploring the Christian faith? Most likely you expressed an openness to learning and a sensitivity to the Holy Spirit. Some particular issue would surface—in you or your environment—and you'd need to pay attention to what God was saying, what he might want you to learn or deal with, or what he seemed to be leading you to focus on next.

It's the same thing now in developing leadership skills. As you lead, consider what circumstances God is placing in your path. How might he want you to grow? What might he want you to learn? Although we're emphasizing leadership skills in this book, we cannot overstate

> As you lead, consider what circumstances God is placing in your path. How might he want you to grow? What might he want you to learn?

the importance of being guided by the Spirit in all the ways we are growing.

Take some time to consider this now in your own life. As you look around, what do you see God doing? How could you join him in that? What is the vision he already has out there that you could be part of? Engage in listening prayer, and in talking with others. As you see where God is already at work, you may gain a sense of how he wants you to contribute to that work and what he wants you learn.

Never forget the spiritual dimension of leadership. Many of you who are regular readers of leadership books will default to focusing on the skills and put the spiritual dimension on the back burner. That's one of the reasons I will end every chapter with a prayer guide with some suggested themes for reflection and prayer. We all need that reminder that leadership skills alone, without the work of the Holy Spirit, will yield us nothing.

> If I speak in the tongues of men or of angels, but do not have love, I am only a resounding gong or a clanging cymbal. If I have the gift of prophecy and can fathom all mysteries and all knowledge, and if I have a faith that can move mountains, but do not have love, I am nothing. If I give all I possess to the poor and give over my body to hardship that I may boast, but do not have love, I gain nothing (1 Cor. 13:1–3).

A vision for the integration of discipleship and leadership

Imagine if all leaders in the church were rooted in this kind of deep, identity-shaping discipleship. What if we all lived out of our walk with Jesus and made disciples of others—and if those people made disciples of yet others?

That's the mandate Jesus gave us in Matthew 28:18–20:

> *Then Jesus came to them and said, "All authority in heaven and on earth has been given to me. Therefore go and make disciples of all nations, baptizing them in the name of the Father and of the Son and of the Holy Spirit, and teaching them to obey everything I have commanded you. And surely I am with you always, to the very end of the age."*

That's what I've been working toward my whole adult life. My vision is to see every person living, growing, and multiplying together as disciples of Jesus who demonstrate the kingdom of God among all peoples. Toward that end, my life's work is to catalyze leaders to accelerate their movement toward this vision.

If we—many of us leaders—are empowered by the Spirit, groups of disciples will start forming. These groups of disciples will form churches, and we will have to begin dealing with all of the leadership issues connected to that numerical reality. We can see how this reality was lived out in the past by reading Acts and the New Testament, and by seeing what the apostles and other early church leaders did.

If we really do discipling well—if we see the Spirit poured out, if we see lives changing—we will have to develop leaders in order to retain and maximize the fruit for the kingdom.

The change starts with us. Personal transformation precedes organizational transformation. Effective leaders are growing, fruitful disciples, connected with God and abiding in Christ. That spirituality permeates effective leadership. Only when we have experienced

> **The change starts with us. Personal transformation precedes organizational transformation.**

personal and ongoing transformation can we hope to lead our churches and ministries toward corporate organizational transformation.

Prayer guide

- What is the vision for which you are praying? Describe it aloud, or in writing to God.

- How can you cultivate a foundation of discipleship in your church or ministry? Who could help you with that?

- If you implemented a strong discipleship process, what leadership problems would be solved? What challenges would you still face?

- How does God want you to grow in your own discipleship? How will you respond to the promptings of the Spirit?

For further reading:

- *The Emotionally Healthy Leader: How Transforming Your Inner Life Will Deeply Transform Your Church, Team, and the World,* by Peter Scazzero

- *Deep Change: Discovering the Leader Within,* by Robert E. Quinn

- *Leadership Prayers,* by Richard Kriegbaum

YOUR OWN PERSONAL DEVELOPMENT

Don't Skip This Chapter

Very early on in my ministry when I was an intern, I was frequently late for staff meetings. Eventually, my supervisor took me aside and said, "You're not late because you didn't run fast enough. You're late because you didn't start early enough." That was one of my early lessons in time management... and in personal development.

Sometimes people don't connect the so-called "practical skills"—things like managing your time and money—with deeper character issues. But they are intrinsically related. Where do our actions come from? Our behaviors are rooted in the way we see life, what we value, what we really believe. Actions are a far better indicator of the heart than words.

> *We know that we have come to know him if we obey his commands. The man who says, "I know him," but does not do what he commands is a liar, and the truth is not in him. But if anyone obeys his word, God's love is truly made complete in him: Whoever claims to live in him must walk as Jesus did (1 John 2:3–6).*

I followed up with that supervisor and in the course of our conversation, he told me something I'll never forget: "When you are late, you're communicating that you're the most important person in the room—and that others can wait for you because you're that important."

> **Actions are a far better indicator of the heart than words.**

Obviously, that was not what I was intending to communicate. I just felt like I was very busy. But he was right; I wasn't respecting other people's time. I was working on the assumption that my to-do list was more important than theirs.

This chapter is about why we all need to start with self-leadership. It's partly a matter of personal discipleship (as addressed in the last chapter), but it's also a matter of modeling behavior for others emulate and getting our own house in order before telling others to do so. Our own personal development is the starting point and essential foundation for developing other leaders.

> *"You hypocrite, first take the plank out of your own eye, and then you will see clearly to remove the speck from your brother's eye" (Matt. 7:5).*

Deal with yourself first before trying to change or grow others. Unless you are modeling a life of discipleship—being transformed personally, growing deeper in your walk with God, and being changed apart from any role you have—you're not ready to lead others. You must first and foremost be a disciple yourself; that foundation is critical. That includes things like having your character shaped, practicing personal integrity,

> **Our own personal development is the starting point and essential foundation for developing other leaders.**

making and keeping promises. These are the areas I addressed in a previous book, *Making Life Count*. As a leader, ask God what needs to change in you personally to get ready for what God wants to do in and through your ministry. Ongoing personal growth is the necessary preparation.

A note from Colin:

Developing as a Christian leader is not only a process—it's a spiritual adventure. I like how Ron Martoia puts it in his book Morph: "God is more interested in customizing His imprint on our soul than he is in building a ministry through us."

Spend a few minutes answering this question: What change (large or small) has the Holy Spirit been prompting you to make in your life to further cultivate a Godly character?

This chapter includes ongoing life management skills, with a particular focus on the areas many leaders really need to zero in on. Topics we'll cover in this chapter include:

- Managing your time
- Setting your priorities
- Learning to say no
- Planning and adjusting
- Managing your money
- Engaging in lifelong learning
- Focusing your personal ministry contribution

> **A note from Colin:**
>
> *Work through the rest of the chapter; it has some good common-sense ideas. But also consider doing an assessment on your strengths and limitations in this area. Spending time working on areas that are already strengths will only frustrate you.*
>
> *One of the best assessments I have used is the Time Mastery Profile® from the Wiley Group. It covers the following areas: Attitudes, Goals, Priorities, Delegation, Procrastination, Analyzing, Planning, Written Communications, Team Time, Scheduling, Interruptions, Meetings.*

Many people, when they move into leadership roles, begin neglecting these issues, forgetting that these issues are ongoing practices rather than one-time fixes. The erosion of these practices of personal development often causes significant leadership problems—so although they are skills for everyone, leaders especially need to stay on top of these skills.

Managing your time

As people gain additional responsibilities as they grow in leadership, it becomes even more challenging to manage time well. A person who may have been strong in time management under normal circumstances may struggle as responsibilities multiply.

Consider the pastor who wakes up one Tuesday morning facing the following to-do items: two scheduled supervisory meetings with staff people, time set aside to work on this week's sermon, a crisis phone call from a member with a daughter in crisis, an action item he told his coach wanted to have done by Friday, a health insurance issue he promised his wife he'd look into, snow to shovel in the driveway before he can leave the house, an inbox full of email, and a commitment to an accountability partner that he'd promised to spend an hour at the gym today.

What should he do? It's a lot to manage. Difficult decisions need to be made, some people will be disappointed, and still not everything will get finished. Here are some helpful strategies for managing your time well:

Track where your time is going. The very first step is to see where your time is currently going. If you do a time audit—recording what you do and how long you do it—for two to four weeks, you should get a relatively accurate picture of where your time is going. Most of the time, the results are surprising. You can then look at how that time usage stacks up against your priorities (see the next section of this chapter).

Create blocks of time. It's hard to get quality, focused work done in little "dribs and drabs." As Peter F. Drucker said, "To have small dribs and drabs of time at your disposal will not be sufficient, even if the total is an impressive number of hours." If you think about bigger blocks of time, then you can protect and prioritize the important things you need to be working on.

Let's say you have a leader training you need to prepare for. Instead of fitting that preparation in on the margins, set aside three two-hour windows over the next couple of weeks. That way, when someone asks you if you can do something at 10 am on Tuesday, you can look at your calendar and see that you already have that time scheduled for leader training preparation. Creating and scheduling blocks of time for priorities can help you protect your time, and focus it on what you have decided is important.

> **Always leave in about a twenty-percent buffer in your calendar, because things come up.**

Leave a twenty-percent buffer. If you schedule yourself for a forty-hour workweek, you'll end up working fifty. Always leave in about a twenty-percent buffer in your calendar, because things come up. Life happens and you'll need the ability to flex with it. If you schedule yourself completely full, you'll still need to find a way to do the overload that comes to you unplanned.

Work off an annual time budget when you need to. Some leadership roles lend themselves to a relatively consistent schedule, while others don't. When you don't have a consistent weekly rhythm, it can be helpful to consider your scheduling in light of an annual time budget. Look at the whole year. You have X number of days off, Y number of holidays, and Z number of working days. Allocate those working days over the course of a year. This approach is especially helpful when you have a role that tends to be seasonal, or when you have extended times of travel for work.

I used this strategy when I was pastoring and doing training/ consulting that involved travel. I also had twelve days a year set aside for planting churches out of my own church. I decided to take a (very) part-time position helping to oversee church planting for my denomination, and then use those twelve days toward denominational church planting.

That seemed like an even trade-off... until I looked at the results after a year. Church planting had gone down significantly. When I looked at how I had spent those twelve days, I realized that ten of them had gone toward mandatory meetings. So even though I had invested the same amount of time, I had effectively lost ten days of productive church planting work.

Even though those meetings were important, I determined that this role wouldn't be a good use of my time because of the other commitments I had. It would be better to use the church planting time directly on getting more churches launched from our own church.

The idea is to carve out annually how many days you're spending on what commitments, then analyze that investment to be sure it reflects your priorities and you can do everything you need to do. In my case, I needed to step down from that position and go back to planting churches out of our own church.

There's no one right answer all the time. Different seasons of life may hold different priorities. But how to use our time most effectively is a question we need to be asking regularly. God has given us only a certain number of years here on this earth, and we are responsible to steward them well. If we're not intentional about how we use our time, it gets away from us. We end up wasting it, or using it on things that don't really reflect our priorities.

Top 10 Principles of Time Management

1. Establish measurable goals and plans.

2. Know how you spend your time.

3. Identify and eliminate time wasters.

4. Know yourself.

5. Take time to plan and set priorities.

6. Learn to say no.

7. Delegate! Delegate! Delegate!

8. Group similar activities together.

9. Organize files/data for easy retrieval.

10. Use a calendar and a to-do list.

Setting your priorities

The key, then, is to discern what's truly important to you and using your time accordingly. The more you grow in your personal discipleship and in your leadership, the more intentional you need to be about reflecting on where you are, what God is doing, and how you can best cooperate with that. For instance, in one season of your leadership you may feel God calling you to give a special emphasis to church health; in another season, outreach.

Setting aside regular time for reflection and reevaluation can help the discernment process. Another tool I've found essential is dialoguing with a coach periodically to help reset my priorities. Even though I am a coach myself, I still need someone to bounce ideas off and to get perspective from, to keep me on a track that's both healthy and productive. (You can read more specifics about coaching and how it works in chapter 4.)

Learning to say no

Knowing your priorities will require saying "no" sometimes. That skill can be a difficult one for ministry leaders, but it's essential. Like any other skill, it requires practice. Sometimes the answer is a "not yet"—you can't do it right now, but it *is* something you would like to do eventually. In that case, an appropriate response might be, "I can't this week, but I'd be happy to do that next week. I have Tuesday and Thursday afternoons open."

In other cases, you may just respond, "I can't meet then. I have a previous commitment." If you have used the block time schedule described earlier in this chapter, that will be true. The time in question may be set aside for sermon preparation, family time, or exercise. Sometimes you will want to move that schedule around if a priority issue comes up and the other person can't meet any other time. If you had planned on taking a bike ride at 8 am and meet with people in the afternoon, but the only time someone could meet is in the morning, you may be able to flip time slots. Sometimes simple rearrangements can still get all the core components finished.

Other times, you just need to say no. "I'm sorry, but I don't have enough bandwidth at this point to take this on and do a good job with it." Practice different ways of saying no to make it easier when the time comes. Too many ministry leaders burn themselves out by saying yes to every request, but not taking time for themselves or their priorities.

Planning and adjusting

Knowing our priorities and aligning our schedule with them doesn't mean that random things won't continue to come up to vie for our attention. (See the previous section, recommending a twenty-percent buffer.) We can prayerfully build a plan by reviewing our commitments, refocusing our priorities, and then proactively scheduling our calendar accordingly.

When the unexpected occurs, we can then engage in a sorting process. Is this unexpected event a distraction—or is it a divine appointment? We need to decide whether this is something we need to refocus our attention on. Say a pastor has Tuesday mornings set aside

> When the unexpected occurs, we can then engage in a sorting process. Is this unexpected event a distraction—or is it a divine appointment?

for sermon preparation. She gets a call for pastoral care. In some cases, it may be an emergency and she needs to go to the hospital right away. In other cases, she may ask if they could meet Tuesday afternoon instead.

The same principle holds true in scenarios when new things come up. We need to continue to decide whether to say yes or no. Sometime a new opportunity may be good, but it doesn't align with your current priorities. In that case you'll likely say no. A different opportunity might be precisely what's needed in order to move forward. You'll need to be able to run new requests through a decision-making grid to figure out the best response. Is it more important than what you're already doing? Is it a God-initiated scheduling change? If so, flex with it and change course. If not, don't.

> *There is a time for everything, and a season for every activity under the heavens (Eccl. 3:1).*

Managing your money

Managing money is a lot like managing time; we have a limited amount of it and what we choose to do with it shows where our priorities lie. Handling our money well is a basic tenet of discipleship. As Jesus said in Matthew 6:21, "For where your treasure is, there your heart will be also." In fact, he talked a lot about money.

God has given us all we have, including the ability to earn money. We are expected to steward well what we have been given. It's a reflection of our character. We are also expected not to make an idol of money—or of the perceived security it brings us.

Below are some general principles for handling our money well, which are applicable for all believers. As leaders, we are to set an example for others as we live faithfully in this area.

Giving: We need to begin with a heart of generosity—a heart that reflects God's heart toward us. Everything belongs to God, and he has only entrusted us with it for a time. As a result, we should be wisely generous, blessing others as God has blessed us.

My strategy:

Here's the plan I have followed since early on in my ministry: First, I give a ten-percent tithe off top of my income. Next, I pay taxes. Then with the money left, I divide it 10/70/20. Ten percent goes to long-term savings, such as retirement. Seventy percent we live on—groceries, housing, etc. Twenty percent goes toward debt removal or an emergency fund—something we could use to pay for unexpected expenses. Even though I have had to live below the level I might have otherwise lived, this system has worked exceptionally well for me in the long term.

Saving: After we have given our firstfruits back to God, we should set some aside to save. We never know what crisis may come our way, and we should do our best to be as prepared as we are able. Set aside a regular amount to save each month and put it aside, unless there is a true emergency.

Spending: With what we do spend, we should spend wisely and with joy and gladness. This is the money we use for our home and food and family and clothing. We need to distinguish between needs and wants, cover the needs first, and afterward we may be able to cover some of the wants. A budget laid out in advance will help immensely with making those kinds of decisions.

> Contentment is not dependent on how much we have, but is an attitude of the heart: thankfulness.

Be content: In all things, we must be content. It's easy to be discontent with what we have, always wanting more. But by focusing on what we do have—on what God has entrusted to us and how we can use it for his kingdom—we can gain a better, more accurate perspective. Contentment is not dependent on how much we have, but is an attitude of the heart: thankfulness.

These are general rules for all disciples. So how is handling money any different for leaders?

We must have a strong foundation of personal financial management, in order to be able to be trusted with managing ministry money. We'll be addressing issues such as ministry budgets and best practices in a later chapter, but handling our personal finances well is a prerequisite for handling ministry money.

Even if we managed responsibly before we came into a position of leadership, certain challenges can make it more difficult. First of all, the whirlwind busyness and stress of ministry makes it easy for us to take our eyes off the ball. Much money management comes down to knowing how much we are spending and on what. If we don't keep track of that, it can begin to feel as if there's money flying out the window, and that we don't really know how much is going out or where it's landing.

Also, in many circles there is a certain pressure to look successful in ministry. Even if you do not come from a health-and-wealth gospel perspective (which I would maintain is really no gospel at all), it can be easy to fall into the trap of wanting to look successful so that we can be taken more seriously. This challenge is especially pronounced if we are ministering to those who are relatively well-off. Yet managing our money responsibility while in leadership is essential—and much more productive than simply trying to appear successful to others.

When I was just beginning to plant a church, I was living on a subsistence salary for the area of was working in. I don't mean to say that I was poor—this was nothing compared to true poverty—just that money was very tight at that time. Janet and I were spending on a cash basis only, using an envelope system to track our money—one envelope for giving, one for saving, one for the mortgage payment, one for groceries, and so on.

I had a very small amount budgeted for clothing each month, and at the time I had a pair of shoes that had holes in the soles. I wasn't about to put new shoes on credit—as I wouldn't have been able pay them off at the time the bill would be due—so I decided that for the time being I'd just keep my feet on the floor during meetings. I was perfectly content with my holey shoes—they weren't so bad as to be ruining my socks—but I didn't want to embarrass God, especially since I was serving in a population that almost across the board didn't have holes in their shoes.

I patiently kept waiting and adding a little money each month to my clothing envelope to save for a new pair of shoes. When I finally had enough to go in to the shoe store, I asked the salesperson for a pair of shoes that would last. I went home with a pair of wingtips; they were already out of style, but they wear like iron. I wore wingtips for many years throughout my pastoral ministry, as a reminder of living within my means and saving and being content.

In reality, one of the biggest ways we can lose credibility in the eyes of the world and in the eyes of those we are ministering to is to mismanage our money, especially in ways that highlight our greed or idolatry. People of any faith background or no faith background generally can clearly see that someone does not have their spiritual life in order if they are worshipping money. Ministries fall because of such problems.

Engaging in lifelong learning

In a similar way as money, our attitude toward learning says a lot about how we see ourselves and how we want others to see us. Are we open to learning new things? Humble about what we do know? Willing to consider alternate perspectives? Or do we feel the need to always be right?

When we do this, our conversations become competitions. Rather than a means to grow and learn, they become only a means for trying to best the other participants—the goal being to look smarter than the next person. What do we come away with? Pride, but no new learning. And no new learning means we are bound to continue repeating our previous mistakes.

What are some helpful ways to open yourself up to lifelong learning and humility? Here are some ideas:

- Scheduling times of reflection
- Asking yourself what you are learning from your present situation
- Processing learnings with others
- Journaling about your learnings
- Becoming a part of a small group of people learning together (a cohort, a study group)
- Trying something new and unfamiliar
- Pushing yourself to grow in an area that is uncomfortable for you
- Reading about ideas that come from a different perspective from your own
- Taking a class or online webinar
- Asking the opinions of others, especially those who think differently than you
- In all conversations, taking a posture of learning

A note from Colin:

This list of ideas for lifelong learnings is based on the following competencies:

- *Self-awareness: The capacity for introspection and learning from experience and mistakes; to not be defensive and to take feedback well, making changes to improve over time; constantly seeking feedback from others in order to keep improving*

- *Critical-thinking skills: The capacity to think deeply and broadly about issues, challenges, or problems, and to develop ways of finding potential solutions that work; measuring the impact of change and making adjustments accordingly*

- *Empathy with people: Creating a climate for caring, warm, and empathetic communication to take place, and demonstrating an understanding of the other person's viewpoint and feelings*

- *Feedback-receiving skills: The capacity to successfully take constructive feedback or accept direct feedback from others without defensiveness; to be able to thank the feedback-giver for new information, even if it is critical or hard to take*

- *Perception/judgment skills: Synthesizing what is seen, heard, or sensed, in order to form a clear view of what may be viable and practical as a possible course of action*

- *Adaptability: Responding positively and quickly to change; constantly making small or large adjustments in what you need to say or do in order to better handle change, either personally or for the team*

A major temptation of leaders is that, as we become teachers of others, we stop being learners. No matter how many years of seminary we have completed, how much Bible reading, how much ministry experience, we all have more to learn. True learning is not only academic: it is experiential, spiritual, and communal.

Ministry leaders who are truly secure in Christ are free to take a posture of openness. We know we're no better than the next person, and in fact assume we have much to learn from the next person, no matter who he or she is.

I've spent many years volunteering in recovery communities. They are often drab and sometimes run-down-looking places where people go who are just not able to function in day-to-day life. Often they are facing issues of addictions, abuse, mental illness, and broken relationships. There's no pretending they have it all together. Therefore, it can be easy for me to go in with a sense of superiority, thinking I know more than they do.

> **Ministry leaders who are truly secure in Christ are free to take a posture of openness.**

A few years back I was giving a brief presentation on living life as God intended, and we broke off into smaller groups to talk about how to apply the lesson. Roger (not his real name) was in my group. Roger is always quiet and doesn't say much. He usually sits a bit away from the rest of the group. On this particular evening we were talking about Micah 6:8: "He has shown you, O mortal, what is good. And what does the Lord require of you? To act justly and to love mercy and to walk humbly with your God."

Roger was staring out the window—probably daydreaming or zoning out, I assumed. In an attempt to draw in his attention, I asked, "Roger, what are you thinking about?" He said, "Well, I was just thinking that last night I was being stingy. It was about a piece of cake. The way I acted, I was being stingy and selfish. My father told me a long time ago never to be stingy."

Although I had assumed not much was going on, God was working with Roger on a very deep character level. He was going beyond just the emotion he felt to a much deeper place. He was responding to the spirit of God. It was amazing to see Roger processing at a deeper spiritual level than I generally do in my own life. At least I had the sense enough to be quiet and not get in the way. The other people in the circle were tearing up; they saw the depths of what he was dealing with.

It was a humbling experience for me. We were on sacred ground, and I recognized that the spiritual sensitivity of the people there is just as great—if not greater—than most of ours in ministry. I realized that I had much to learn from them.

For by the grace given me I say to every one of you: Do not think of yourself more highly than you ought, but rather think of yourself with sober judgment, in accordance with the faith God has distributed to each of you (Rom. 12:3).

Focusing your personal ministry contribution

Leaders are not "one size fits all." We come with different experiences, passions, and gifts. No one can do everything—and none of us should try. There's an endless list of good things to do, but if we try to spread ourselves too thin we won't be able to accomplish any of them. Therefore, each of us needs to focus on what God has for us to contribute specifically, or we will become scattered in our efforts.

Each leader will bring something unique to the table. "For we are God's handiwork, created in Christ Jesus to do good works, which God prepared in advance for us to do" (Eph. 2:10). Consider your own abilities. How has God uniquely gifted you? How might he want to use you? He has given each of us the strength and giftings necessary for the contributions he wants us to make.

When we reflect on our lives, experiences, interests, and passions, our contribution shouldn't be much of a mystery. *Finding a Job You*

Love, by Arthur Miller and Ralph Mattsen, walks people through the process of reflecting on their lives to identify achievements that were significant to them. Then the book helps readers unpack those achievements and look for common threads. The idea is that God places within us the motivation to do a certain kind of work. I took a few days alongside my wife Janet to work through this book together, and it was an eye-opening experience. Even things I hadn't thought were connected to my current calling were connected.

When we are younger, we try new things, and those experiences shape us. Over time it becomes clearer what God wants to accomplish through us. Eventually, when that picture solidifies more, leaders should try to make sure at least seventy percent of what they are doing is in areas of strength and calling. From there, we can work toward eighty percent, but any less than sixty percent probably won't be tenable for very long.

It's okay if you are a leader but aren't gifted in, say, administration. Bring someone in to help you with that. The same holds true for other areas of weakness. We need to bring in other people and rely on them for their contribution. Often we will, however, need to reach a basic level of competency. For me, shepherding and pastoral care can be a challenge, and I have repeatedly brought in help. I care about people, but I'm not a natural at how to best show it. So even while bringing in help, I have asked myself, "What are three things I can do to be strategic in this area? How could I improve if I did only these three things consistently?" I may never be excellent at pastoral care, but I can (and did) develop basic competence.

> It's easy to get wrapped up in all that needs to be done, but we need to be able to see the bigger picture.

Later in life, calling seems to crystallize more clearly for most people. When we can look back over a longer track record, we can see our accomplishments and our contributions. Especially if you are leading a ministry at that point, this can be a good time to step back and take stock. It's easy to get wrapped up in all that needs to be done, but we need to be able to see the bigger picture.

We also need to be able to focus our efforts on working *on* the ministry rather than just *in* the ministry. For instance, you have a bunch of tasks that need to be done—and at the beginning of a ministry, your own name is probably on all of those tasks. But as you grow the organization and develop others, you begin being able to write other people's names on some of those tasks. You're then not doing all the work of the ministry, but focusing your efforts on growing the ministry itself and moving it forward.

Being strategic in where you focus your efforts and your contributions can have significant payoff for your organization down the road. Find the one thing God wants you to do, and then do it. Keep your focus there. If it's developing new leaders, zero in on that. If it's planting and multiplying churches, focus your energy on that. The more you grow as a leader, the more intentional you need to be about reflecting on where you are, what God's doing, and how you can cooperate.

> ### A note from Colin:
>
> *Most Christian leaders have a ministry description they have to follow, whether it is formal or informal. You will always know when you have strayed from it because someone will tell you.*
>
> *It is always prudent to work out the basic requirements of that description, and then do what Lyle Schaller called "pay the rent." This can usually be achieved in about three days per week if a church has less than two hundred people. Once this is accomplished, you have discretionary time to focus on your personal ministry contribution. Start small and slowly add time to this area. (By the way, if you believe you can't pay the rent in three days it's time to review your time management.)*

> **Find the one thing God wants you to do and then do it. Keep your focus there.**

Conclusion

Ongoing personal development is crucial for leaders. When we stop growing, or when our lives get out of balance and we don't deal with it, we end up leading in ways that fail and that can even be harmful to ourselves or those around us. Our actions are what those around us will see and emulate.

> *Show me your faith without deeds, and I will show you my faith by my deeds.... You see that his faith and his actions were working together, and his faith was made complete by what he did (James 2:18, 22).*

When we as leaders have addressed the logs in our own eyes, then we are ready to be able to help others with the specks in their eyes, both through our words and our deeds. We are also then ready to put together an effective team, which is the subject of the next chapter.

Prayer guide

- What have you been sensing from God as you've read this chapter?

- Which areas do you feel most strong in?

- What's one area in which you need to grow?

- How can you put this scripture into practice right now: "First take the plank out of your own eye, and then you will see clearly to remove the speck from your brother's eye" (Matt. 7:5)?

- What action steps will you take to respond to the Spirit's prompting?

For further reading:

- *Getting Things Done: The Art of Stress-Free Productivity,* by David Allen

- *Making Life Count: Following Jesus in the 21st Century,* by Robert E. Logan and Tara Miller

- *Finding a Job You Can Love,* by Ralph T. Mattson and Arthur F. Miller

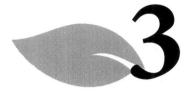

WHO DO YOU NEED?

Getting the Right Players on Your Team

When I was pastoring a church, I taught a membership class. It included general information about the church, as well as teaching on spiritual gifts and direction on how to get involved. A woman named Iris took the class, which was an eight-week series. After the last class, she came up to me and said, "Bob, this class was excellent. I learned so much and grew so much. It was really helpful to me. Could I give you some feedback?"

"Sure."

"This class was horribly disorganized."

She was right; I recognized the truth of what she said immediately. I'm decent at winging it, but I'd been making up the class as I went, bringing in random handouts each week, without a clear idea of next steps. But then Iris continued, "Could I help you fix that?"

For the next few weeks, Iris met with me for fifteen to twenty minutes each Monday. By asking me a series of questions, she came away with a hit list of tasks she was going to accomplish that week. One week it might be interviewing a certain group of people.

The next week it might be putting together a coherent notebook for the course. The next it might be developing a feedback system to discover other areas that needed improvement.

Iris was a mother of preschoolers—a stay-at-home mom in search of a challenge. She wanted something different from the challenges of stay-at-home parenting, yet something she could do at the same time, so Iris became a ministry organizer for me.

I am a catalyzer: I love to start new things. Iris could come in and bring order to the messes I created from the new things started— then they'd work, and I would be free to press on to the next thing. I'd always been able to do a little bit of organizing myself— that's how I got that class off the ground in the first place—but not enough to make it truly functional. I needed Iris on my team.

> From him the whole body, joined and held together by every supporting ligament, grows and builds itself up in love, as each part does its work (Eph. 4:16).

I've always said, "If you want to know my weaknesses, look at the strengths of the people around me." I prefer the big picture to the details. I've gotten better at managing the important details over time—I've had to—but it's never been an area of strength for me. Inevitably things fall through the cracks. So at various seasons of my life I've had some amazing

> If you want to know my weaknesses, look at the strengths of the people around me.

administrative help—people like Iris, truly gifted people who can take a crazy schedule and whip it into a semblance of order. People who can find the document I need for the next meeting before I remember that I needed it. I stand in awe of these people, and they have contributed significantly to every ministry I've been a part of over the years. (Yes, I mean you, Lou, Joan, Michelle, Laura, Rebecca, and Marcy.)

No matter who you are, you can't go it alone. Jesus had all the gifts. None of the rest of us do. Prayerfully discerning who we are and who we need is a critical piece of fruitful ministry. We must pull different strengths together, mobilizing a variety of people around us. Coworkers and team members must be people with a similar vision but complementary skills.

> **A note from Colin:**
>
> *An important starting point as a leader is to know your strengths and limitations as well as you can, but this is not easy to do especially if you are reasonably new in ministry. We usually start with self-evaluation, which can lead us to believe we have a range of mental, spiritual, and physical limitations and restrictions that will inhibit our present and future capacity to lead. Or we may think that we have little or no constraints, only opportunities and possibilities. Only time and application will tell if our thoughts are "real."*

When you know your own strengths, you then need others around you with different strengths. You're all working toward the same vision, but you each have different contributions to make, in order for that vision to become a reality.

Let's take one of my early ministry teams as an example. When I was a junior at UCLA, I took on the middle-school ministry at my church. I was in charge of organizing something called "Come Alive Week," which was basically a jazzed-up Vacation Bible School for older kids. We'd meet every evening for five nights and do all kinds of different activities: go-carts, swimming, music, Bible lessons. We even put together a "sound scavenger hunt," where we took the kids to the UCLA campus with tape recorders and had them go around trying to record specific sounds. The outcome we were aiming for was to establish discipling relationships with these middle-school students.

To put the ministry together, I needed a lot of people in a lot of different roles. Someone would need to facilitate the games; someone would need to do the registration. There were permission slips, name tags, refreshments, worship, teaching, discussion time. I gathered a group of about fifteen college students and we started with a lot of teaching on spiritual gifts. The idea was to help them discover their gifts and to identify gifts they wanted to experiment with, in order to discern which ones they possessed. The focus was not only on getting the job done, but on developing the people serving.

After the training and preparation time, everyone got a role aligned with a gift they wanted to explore: administration, service, hospitality, teaching, encouragement. Some people had very small roles. But the whole team worked together to accomplish the mission.

A note from Colin:

Getting the right players on your team starts with a few general questions:

- *Are you only looking for someone to do a short-term task?*
- *Can they do it by themselves or do they need others?*
- *Are you looking for someone who will work in a specific but longer-term ministry?*
- *How complex is that ministry? How many other people are involved?*
- *Are you planning to work with someone long term and help them to prepare for a more extensive ministry?*

The more extensive the ministry, the more you will need to know the person. Strong observable growing Discipleship Competencies may not be the first priority for a short-term task but they are essential for more extensive ministry roles.

Here are a few important points to consider as you look at how you can most effectively build your team:

- Reflecting on your motivations

- Praying about who to invest in

- Determining what roles you need filled on your team

- Getting the right people on your team

- Using specialized resource people

Reflecting on your motivations

Before you start building a team, consider *why* you want one. Some leaders want a team that will serve them. They can give orders and have a fleet of people ready to carry those orders out. In this case, the team members aren't empowered... just utilized.

I've seen situations like this more than once, and although they may look efficient on the surface, they inevitably result in high burnout, high turnover, and a ministry that is overly dependent on one leader—usually to the point that it can't be replicated or even grow beyond a certain point. And that's not even considering the relational dynamics on such a team, which are unhealthy at best, toxic and destructive at worst. That's hardly what you want to model in a ministry environment.

Part of the reason leaders are drawn to creating a team to serve them is a legitimate desire to get things done. "I don't want to sit around navel-gazing and talking about our personal growth. I want to accomplish things for Jesus!" I can empathize with such a position. I tend to be goal-oriented myself.

Yet I've found that you can get the job done *and* help your team members grow at the same time. I've always had a phrase when leading ministries: If you serve, you will grow. I am committed to your development. It wasn't just about getting people to do a job, but an equal commitment to their development. You can get more and better ministry done if you are also empowering people at the same time. Rather seeing "team development time" taking away from "productive ministry time," see it as the fuel for productive ministry. This investment in your people is what actually gets you where you want to go.

> **Part of the reason leaders are drawn to creating a team to serve them is a legitimate desire to get things done. Yet I've found that you can get the job done *and* help your team members grow at the same time.**

Your commitment to team members, as their leader, is to help them grow into their giftedness as well as help them see how their particular role ties into the bigger picture. How does what they do matter? They need to see that. And they need to see the bigger picture and how they're contributing to it.

What is that bigger picture? When you look to the horizon, it's the harvest fields. So plentiful and vast, stretching beyond where you can see. The needs there are incredible, and sometimes overwhelming. How can you even begin to meet them? Not by yourself (that's for sure), but through developing more workers in the harvest fields. When you develop your team well, that's precisely what you are contributing toward. Your motivation should be both for the harvest to be reached *and* for your team members to grow and develop. The two work together symbiotically.

When he saw the crowds, he had compassion on them, because they were harassed and helpless, like sheep without a shepherd. Then he said to his disciples, "The harvest is plentiful but the workers are few. Ask the Lord of the harvest, therefore, to send out workers into his harvest field" (Matt. 9:36–38).

Praying about who to invest in

Investing in others isn't just about lightening our own load and meeting the needs of the people we already have. It needs to be primarily about raising leaders for the harvest. Anything less than a vision for raising up people to reach more people is too small of a vision. That's the motivation.

As you look toward developing workers for the harvest, who should you be investing in? The answers are not always obvious. Don't limit yourself to investing in people who already seem to be ready to go... or almost ready to go. Take time in prayer. Observe, reflect and discern. Ask God who he might want you to invest in. Ask others you trust to pray with you.

> Don't limit yourself to investing in people who already seem to be ready to go.

Look further into the future—long term, too. Look to those who want to raise up others to increase capacity. You need some leaders who are short-term leaders. But even at this stage, don't neglect bringing on people with future potential. So many senior leaders think only about the immediate need—Who can we get to do what needs to be done right now?—and are not thinking of the longer term. Bringing on potential future leaders now who are in need of development is a way to grow them through their current involvement—and it leads to multiplication potential.

A note from Colin:

Make it a priority to set aside some time to look at how Jesus went about developing leaders who would eventually make a significant impact on the world. Consider how he started, how he went about the development process, how he dealt with the frustrations.

Reflect on how he did it over and against how you do it. Make a mental note of the time it took and don't be in a hurry. The church has become so enamoured with reductionism over the last fifty years that we now accept "little in—not a lot out."

So think of the team members for your immediate needs, but also consider apprentices. Paul and Barnabas had John Mark with them during some of their missionary travels. Although he didn't work out well during the first go-round, he did contribute in the long term. As you pray about who to invest in on your team, think in two categories: people who may be able to contribute in the short term, and people who may be able to contribute in the long term.

Determining what roles you need filled on your team

Consider the functions you need covered on your team. Here are some roles common to many teams, although there are certainly others:

- Idea person—big-picture vision

- Mobilizer or recruiter

- Gatherer

- Administrator

- Financial oversight

- A person with organizational authority

- Communicator

- Intercessor

 What other roles do you need covered? Even if it's not a specific job description, you may need people who fill a certain relational role: an enthusiast who gets everyone excited about the task at hand, or a stabilizing influence who others feel they can always talk to.

And again, remember to connect every task to the bigger vision. Consider the roles of the people on your team. How do their daily tasks contribute to the bigger picture of what your ministry is accomplishing? And as they practice those daily tasks, how are they growing? What new challenges may lie ahead for them? To keep motivated, everyone needs to see how their task ties into the bigger picture.

A note from Colin:

The biggest mistake I encounter in my work as a consultant/ coach is nicely summed up by Simon Sinek in his book Start with Why. *Sinek states that we make most of our structural discussions (like what roles need to be filled) on what we do or how we do it, and these decisions are based on the past (usually denominational history). That's fine, as long as the what and how are behaviorally connected to the why. Why do we exist? What is the bigger picture of our purpose?*

If you are not leading out of the why, then you are managing out of the what and how. More on this later.

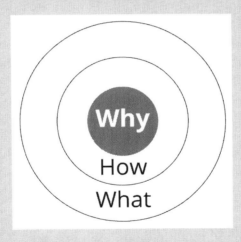

Getting the right people on your team

Once you are clear on roles, how do you find and develop the right people to fill them? Certainly these people must be gifted for the roles you need on the team—although you will still need to develop and support them. But also look toward character qualities.

What qualities should you look for? One of my favorite answers to this question comes from Ray Stedman (www.raystedman.org): "a searching mind, a humble heart, an evident gift, and a faithful spirit." Consider each of these characteristics in turn.

- A searching mind means someone who is curious and interested in learning. She has enough initiative to seek out new ideas and challenges. Sometimes people just need to try out new things to discover their giftedness. The Bible commands us to teach, serve, encourage, and give anyway— we may as well pay attention to where we might be gifted as we live in obedience.

- The second quality, a humble heart, is related: Not only is she curious but she is teachable. She doesn't assume she already has all the answers, but is willing to take correction, learn, and grow.

- An evident gift means there is some evidence of effectiveness in ministry. Roles she has served in the past have borne some fruit, and others can testify to her natural ability. The gifts may be undeveloped, but they are evident.

- The final quality is a faithful spirit. For this quality, we also look to the past. When she has made commitments in the past, has she kept them to the best of her ability? Has she followed through and done what she said she would do?

These four qualities are the basic essentials that everyone needs, regardless of their specific goal on the team.

Depending on your specific ministry, you'll also want to assess a potential team member's alignment with the values and vision (which we'll unpack more in the next chapter). For instance, if your ministry is all about serving and reaching teenagers and the person you're evaluating doesn't enjoy engaging with them, the team may not be a good fit for him even if he possesses all four of the qualities above. Yet think creatively—it's possible someone may not enjoy engaging with teenagers himself but does have a heart for reaching them. Possibly that person could provide support for adults on the team.

Allow some flexibility on team formation and direction, especially if your ministry is young or broadly based like a local church, which will likely incorporate many different ministries. Although your team members must be on board with the general direction you're going, they will also help you shape your values, vision, and mission as the organization grows. In that sense, there's a bit of a chicken-and-egg dynamic. (For more about this concept of the ministry growing and changing shape over time, see chapter 11 on organizational development.)

One important mistake to avoid: Don't pick people just like yourself. You'll need a wide variety of gifts, abilities, and personalities on your team. You don't need more yous—you need people who are different from you: people

> **You need people who are different from you: people with the capacity for leadership, yet people with different strengths and gifts from your own.**

with the capacity for leadership, yet people with different strengths and gifts from your own. In this way, you can create a team that is complementary and diverse. Imagine a ship with everyone trying to be the navigator. It doesn't work well, does it?

Also avoid falling into the trap of putting people on your team that you'd be friends with. If you happen to become friends at some point, great. But sometimes the people you enjoy being around recreationally are not the same people you work together best with. Certainly aim for people you can get along with, but your team doesn't need to be made up of your social group.

As Paul Ford wrote in his book *Moving from I to We*, "Where are you powerful, how are you weak, and who do you need?" When we know our contribution, we need to figure out who we need around us. That's why I said earlier that if you want to know what my weaknesses are, look at the strengths of the people around me and you'll have a pretty good idea.

Finally, don't be afraid to choose strong people to work with. You may not always agree with them, but you do need people who challenge you to see things differently. Having a crew of yes-men around you can appear to be a harmonious team, but if you want actual health you need people who aren't afraid to stand up to you and discuss different perspectives.

Using specialized resource people

Sometimes for optimal team functioning you will also need specialized resource people—experts in a particular area. They may not be people who are technically on your team—more like pinch-hitters. Maybe you need a professional musician or an outside consultant or a website designer. Consider any of those needs you may have. Who do you know that could help?

These specialized resource people don't need to be paid staff. They can be volunteers or retired people with specific skills or strengths. I once had a man who helped me do research for my sermons. I know of another pastor who had a retired Navy officer helping him with strategic planning. Think broadly: Do you need a tax person, a bookkeeper, a virtual administrative assistant? Sometimes there are people right around you who can help you. I knew a woman who loved to throw big parties—that was a skill I could definitely put to use. People often don't realize the strengths they have that can be used on a team to make a significant contribution.

Holding people loosely

After all of this work gathering and assembling a great team, there's one more thing you have to do: Let go. Even after you invest time and energy in developing them, God might call them

WHO DO YOU NEED?

on to something else. Although that reality is painful to many senior leaders—and often even seen as a betrayal—it's actually a good reminder that the kingdom is much bigger than just our own church or ministry. God is doing much more in the world.

We can serve as sending organizations, training leaders and sending them out to do important kingdom work. When looked at from the right perspective, that's not a net loss—it's a net gain.

Once a group of us on the pastoral staff team were praying for discernment. The Spirit led us to set apart our associate pastor, Byron, and send him out as a church planter. It was hard because he led our music, was popular in the community, and was a huge support to me. But I had to let him go because that's what God was calling Byron to do: plant a new church.

> Now in the church at Antioch there were prophets and teachers: Barnabas, Simeon called Niger, Lucius of Cyrene, Manaen (who had been brought up with Herod the tetrarch) and Saul. While they were worshiping the Lord and fasting, the Holy Spirit said, "Set apart for me Barnabas and Saul for the work to which I have called them." So after they had fasted and prayed, they placed their hands on them and sent them off (Acts 13:1–3).

I then turned over his role over to Doug, someone I had been investing in and developing for quite a while without knowing exactly why. I just knew God was calling me to invest in him and so I was. Doug then took on Byron's old role of worship pastor.

Two years later, I had another staff person, Rob, who I was working with. He had been a summer intern for a couple of years and then was a full-time staff member. Each year I would pray about how I could develop him further. One year I realized the only way he could continue to develop was to become a senior pastor. Should I send Rob out as a planter too?

THE LEADERSHIP DIFFERENCE   65

I wrestled with the idea for a few months. Then the Lord said, "You're right, Bob. He's ready. You're out of here." Wait—me? *I'm* the one who's out of here?

It turns out that Rob was not called to be a planter, but rather to take over as senior pastor at our current church; I was the one being called somewhere else. Sometimes we may even need to leave our own roles for the sake of continuing to develop someone else. In this case, that was the right call.

In the Body of Christ, we help people find their niche in giftedness and ministry. That extends beyond roles in our own ministry. Sometimes to help people continue growing, God may move them to new places, new roles, or new ministries. While that may be a loss here, it is a kingdom gain... both for the person moving on to the next phase of what God has for them, as well as for those God is calling us to invest in and develop next.

> ### A note from Colin:
>
> *Holding people lightly is a kingdom perspective that is important for those we are developing, but it also highlights the level of our trust in God. If what you are doing is truly from God, then we know He knows the future long before we do.*
>
> *A number of years ago I joined the staff of a growing church. One of the stated beliefs of the senior pastor was "we not only give people away but we always give our best." I watched that church grow to become a megachurch, and I believe this kingdom attitude was one of the reasons it grew. God blesses kingdom action.*

Sometimes to help people continue growing, God may move them to new places, new roles, or new ministries.

---

*So Christ himself gave the apostles, the prophets, the
evangelists, the pastors and teachers, to equip his people
for works of service, so that the body of Christ may be built
up until we all reach unity in the faith and in the knowledge
of the Son of God and become mature, attaining to the whole
measure of the fullness of Christ (Eph. 4:11–13).*

Prayer guide

- What is God saying to you as you read this chapter?

- Who have you found yourself thinking of and praying for?

- Who might God be calling you to develop?

- Consider any people currently on your team. How can you help them develop further?

- How can you pray for others?

- What action steps are you sensing God would have you take?

For further reading:

- *The Five Dysfunctions of a Team: A Leadership Fable,* by Patrick Lencioni

- *Strengths-based Leadership: Great Leaders, Teams, and Why People Follow,* by Tom Rath and Barry Conchie

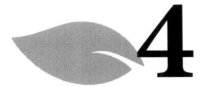

DEVELOPING PEOPLE

Creating a Framework for Growth

No matter what their role, you can develop anyone through coaching. Lou came to my church early on as a brand-new Christian. Shortly afterward, I hired her as my first administrative assistant. I began using a coaching approach with her whenever she came to me with questions.

Lou would come into my office; something had come up and she wanted to know what she should do about it. Instead of answering, I'd ask, "What's the real issue here?" She didn't know, so we'd talk about it and think through how to handle it. The next day she'd come in with another situation that had come up and say, "Here's what came up, here's what I think the real issue is... what do you want me to do." I'd ask, "What principles need to be considered?" She didn't know, so we'd talk about it.

Our conversations began to become a pattern during the last thirty minutes of her workday. Next time Lou would come in and say, "Here's what came up, here's what I think the real issue is, and here are the principles that need to be considered. What should I do?" I would ask, "What options do we have?" And then we'd talk about it. The following day, Lou would come in and say,

"Here's what came up. Here's what I think the real issue is. Here's what principles need to be considered. Here are the options we have. What do you want me to do?" I would ask what her recommendation was.

Finally, we got to the point where Lou would come in and say, "Here's what came up. Here's what I think the real issue is. Here's what principles need to be considered. Here are the options we have. Here's what I'd recommend we do." And I would respond, "What do you need me for?" She would stop and think about it, and respond, "I guess I just wanted to make sure my thinking was sound."

As Lou took on more and more responsibility, she was promoted to become the church's business administrator. At that time, we were constructing a building. She interfaced with contractors and board members to oversee a ten-thousand-square-foot building project. I didn't have to do much at all, and she brought the project in ahead of schedule and under budget.

Although the subject matter was different, Jesus took a similar approach as he developed his disciples. He invested relationally, he provided instruction and support, he traveled alongside them, he challenged them to try things they were uncomfortable with, then he debriefed with them afterward about how it went to help cement the learnings.

> He appointed the twelve—designating them apostles—that
> they might be with him and that he might send them out
> to preach and to have authority to drive out demons (Mark
> 3:14–15).

In Mark 3–5, we see how Jesus spent time with his disciples and taught them. He showed them firsthand how he worked. They witnessed Jesus performing miracles, healings, and casting out demons. They saw his interactions with the teachers of the law, and he explained the meaning of the parables to them in private.

ROBERT E. LOGAN | LOGANLEADERSHIP.COM

Then in Mark 6:7–13, we see Jesus giving the disciples instructions and sending them out on their own for a time:

> Calling the Twelve to him, he sent them out two by two and gave them authority over evil spirits. These were his instructions: "Take nothing for the journey except a staff—no bread, no bag, no money in your belts. Wear sandals, but not an extra tunic. Whenever you enter a house, stay there until you leave that town. And if any place will not welcome you or listen to you, shake the dust off your feet when you leave, as a testimony against them." They went out and preached that people should repent. They drove out many demons and anointed many sick people with oil and healed them.

Jesus gave them the information and instructions they needed when they needed them: just in time, just enough, and not too much.

A note from Colin:

The "just-in-time" approach of Jesus was often built around the questions of the disciples. When a person is ministering and facing a situation that is new to them, their level of openness is usually very strong. They are looking for the how with some why.

Have you ever wondered how we got to the other side of the pendulum swing, where we believe development happens by removing people from doing ministry and using a "just-in-case" approach which has no immediate application? A move to a lot of why and little how. If this is your approach, ask yourself the question, "How is it working for you and your leaders?"

> Jesus gave them the information and instructions they needed when they needed them: just in time, just enough, and not too much.

How could you use a similar process developing leadership skills in others in your ministry? Unless you want to be doing all the ministry all by yourself forever (which I most definitely do not recommend), you'll need to develop others. You'll need to find a way to orient and then guide your people along the way toward their particular goals.

Consider all the different areas of ministry where you may want to develop leadership skills in others: children's ministry, small group leaders, service and outreach teams, worship team, teaching, administration and management, event planning, discipleship initiatives, compassion ministry... the list is infinite. Whatever the specific ministry area, you can use the same basic framework to begin developing your people to their maximum potential.

What you need is not a list of all the specific skills for all the possible ministries—what you need is a principle-based process that you can adapt for each specific need. Although we'll go into much more depth in chapter 10 on advanced people development, we're starting here with the basic development of people through coaching. No matter who someone is or what their role, you can help develop them through a coaching approach. Think of it as the skill-development edge of disciplemaking. How can you take a disciple—wherever he or she currently is—and challenge them to take the next step?

In this chapter, we'll first discuss how to create a culture conducive to growth, and then we'll lay out a six-step framework that provides a flexible process for people development.

Creating cultures of growth

First you need to create a culture that encourages and supports growth. There are three basic components to this type of culture. Consider your ministry context, and make sure you are providing enough structure and support in each of these areas to truly help people grow.

- **Environments**: New leaders need a designated ministry environment in which to practice their new skills. This could be a small group, a new worship service, or a specific outreach initiative. It's basically a practice field—a place where people can try out new skills and see how it goes. Creating safe environments in which to experiment, try, and sometimes fail is crucial to people's development.

- **Relationships**: New leaders need a coach as well as peers to help them develop most effectively. Make sure they have someone more experienced to guide them along and challenge them, as well as natural ways to connect with others who are also learning new skills. Making these relational connections will go a long way toward making your people-development process effective and supportive.

- **Processes**: New leaders need a clear hands-on process (such as the one described earlier in this chapter), in order to develop their new skills. When they are just beginning something new, by definition they don't know what to do. Make it clear. Tell them where to start and what to work on first, then where to go from there. Having a clear process already in place will free people up to learn.

A note from Colin:

All the way through this book Bob refers to coaching. If you are not using a coaching structure in your ministry, then find out more about it and implement it. If you are the leader of a small church you will find it helpful. If your church is growing, or it is mid-sized or larger, then it is essential.

Staffing for growth is still important, but can you afford the old twentieth-century view of this? Create a culture that encourages and supports the involvement of more and more of the congregation. If you believe this won't work because people don't have time these days, you need to realize that you don't have a time problem—you either have a discipleship problem or an insufficient vision problem.

A process for development

Here's a process of how you can go about developing and supporting those in your ministry, in order to develop them. I've laid out this process in much more depth in my previous book *From Followers to Leaders* (coauthored with Tara Miller), but have provided a basic overview here for your reference. Although this people-development process may look a bit different in different situations, these six basic steps apply to developing people in any area of ministry. It's essentially an on-the-job training process.

> **Creating safe environments in which to experiment, try, and sometimes fail is crucial to people's development.**

1) Find the right people to develop. You only have a limited amount of time and energy, so you want to invest it where it will do the most good. Jesus chose twelve to invest in. How many do you have the capacity to invest in? Most leaders, depending on their workload and job description, would say between three and six.

Next, consider who those people should be. Whose development is God calling you to invest in? Take time to pray and discern. Look around you. Listen for the direction of the Holy Spirit.

What qualities are you looking for in those you want to invest in? I'd recommend the following, although you may have others you also consider important:

- Currently living as a disciple

- Teachability

- Demonstrated interest in the ministry area

2) Talk about where they want to go. Once you have a sense of who God may be leading you to invest in, see if he's leading that person in the same direction. Talk with her; open up a discussion. Ask her how she wants to grow, where she envisions herself serving and leading in the future. Tell her what you've been thinking, being as specific as possible. For example, say, "It seems to me that you might be good at coordinating events for newcomers at our church. I've noticed your heart for getting new people connected, as well as your significant administration skills. Is this a ministry area you'd be interested in developing your skill set for?"

Give her time to think about it; the idea may be new to her. Discernment is not a one-sided process. If she declines your offer of development in this area, God likely has something different in mind for her. You might be able to point her to someone else who can develop her in a different area. In that case, go back to step one: finding the right people to develop. Don't allow immediate ministry needs to push you into the corner of feeling you have to get someone in that slot right now, whether the person fits or not. Make sure she knows how you are offering to help develop her skills, and take time to be sure it's in a direction in which she wants to go as well.

> **Don't allow immediate ministry needs to push you into the corner of feeling you have to get someone in that slot right now, whether the person fits or not.**

3) *Help them get started.* Sometimes the hardest part is getting started. Say the person you're developing wants to learn how to lead in a small-group setting. What should he do? Where should he begin? Some churches throw people in the deep end, where many drown before they learn. Other churches have extensive training programs, most of which are classroom-based and specialize in answering questions people haven't thought of yet.

What I recommend is a brief orientation and a clearly staked-out environment. First, the orientation should tell this new leader just the basics of what he is expected to do and why. What is the broader purpose of this ministry? What are the basic responsibilities? Who should he ask if he needs help?

Then he'll need an environment in which to practice. Make it a smaller environment with clear limits—after all, it's better to learn how to swim in a shallow pool than in the ocean. Since he wants to lead a small group, maybe try placing him in one where he can observe and help, rather than expecting him to start his own from scratch. In this kind of environment, there is supervision and help. He can learn to facilitate the prayer time. He can practice leading the discussion time. Eventually he may need to try out some conflict resolution or organize a service project for the group. The point is to create an environment for hands-on, real-life experiential learning.

4) Provide coaching along the way. Too often we give prospective new leaders a ministry role and turn them loose without support. What they need after taking on a ministry role is a point person they can talk with as they get started. There will inevitably be questions, barriers, problems, choices, and they will need someone to bounce ideas off of. "How do I handle X?" "What should I do about Y?"

I call this person a coach. The best coaches listen and ask questions to help people think through the specific situations they're dealing with. They aren't teachers, although they sometimes can point people to helpful resources. They aren't experts, although sometimes they will have a helpful perspective. Primarily, coaches are especially important when people are just getting started in ministry.

Make sure every new ministry leader has a coach to meet with at least once a month to reflect on how the ministry is going, along with questions, learnings, and other insights.

5) Connect them with peers. As anyone who's been involved with a support group of some kind knows, there's just no substitute for being able to talk with people who understand experientially— people who get what you're going through because they are right there in it with you. Whether it's a group of new moms, an

Alcoholics Anonymous group, or a gathering of first-year Sunday school teachers, these are the people who understand the joys and the challenges.

Peers fulfill a different role from the coach. The coach, although helpful, is likely not dealing with the same challenges right now. Peers are. They help other new leaders remember that they aren't in it alone. A good group of peers binds people together to provide support that is stronger than just one person alone.

> Also, if two lie down together, they will keep warm.
> But how can one keep warm alone?
> Though one may be overpowered,
> two can defend themselves.
> A cord of three strands is not quickly broken (Eccl. 4:11–12).

Build in natural times for new leaders to talk with one another and connect for relationship and support. Many ministry leaders assume that one of the most helpful things for new leaders is new content; so when they bring their new leaders together, the instinct is to provide training. But you'd be amazed at how helpful it is to bring, say, a group of eight ministry leaders together—with zero new content—and let them discuss these five questions, then pray for one another:

- What's working?

- What's not working?

- What are you learning?

- What needs to change?

- What's next?

Try it and see. Listen to the people afterward rave about how helpful and beneficial that time was—even though you provided no answers and no new content.

6) Celebrate success. An important component in both the coaching relationship and within the peer network is celebration. New leaders who are developing their skills tend to focus on what went wrong, what they didn't handle well, what ideas didn't work. They need prompting to celebrate the successes too, even minor ones. For instance, maybe the overall strategy didn't work, but it did yield some unexpected wins. Celebrate those!

As you develop new leaders, be intentional about setting aside time to rest and reflect on what has been accomplished. Validate and reinforce what they've done well. Publicly acknowledge and recognize important contributions. People need celebration all along the way throughout this process. Celebration and affirmation serve as the foundation of all future change and growth.

> *A note from Colin:*
>
> *As a leader, it is important to let individuals and teams know that they are appreciated in concrete and tangible ways. This will be done quite differently, depending on the task and the individuals involved. If a proverbial "pat on the back" is accompanied by a spoken reassurance that the individual is doing well and going in the right direction, the payoff in terms of high morale, effort, and personal growth can be enormous.*
>
> *It is also important to match the degree of praise to the size and nature of the accomplishment. Minor recognition for major achievements, and major recognition for a minor contribution, may send confusing messages.*

Celebration and affirmation serve as the foundation of all future change and growth.

Only after taking time for rest and celebration should you turn new leaders' vision toward what's next. What do they sense God calling them to now? How can they continue growing and stretching? Who might they need to team with or connect with? Sometimes it's necessary to bring additional people on board to expand the current reach of ministry. Who might God be calling them to help develop?

From there, the cycle begins again.

Coaching is one important piece of the process. We want to develop people holistically, intentionally, and with a capacity for growth and multiplication. Doing that means creating a relational environment with processes in place for growth. Consider how the apostle Paul did that during his ministry years in Ephesus:

> Paul entered the synagogue and spoke boldly there for three months, arguing persuasively about the kingdom of God. But some of them became obstinate; they refused to believe and publicly maligned the Way. So Paul left them. He took the disciples with him and has discussions daily in the lecture hall of Tyrannus. This went on for two years, so that all the Jews and Greeks who lived in the province of Asia heard the word of the Lord (Acts 19:8–10).

If you invest the time and energy necessary to develop others, you'll never lack for leaders. In fact, you'll develop leaders and workers for your own ministry and beyond—wherever God calls them.

Prayer guide

- What has stood out most to you as you have read this chapter? What are you hearing from God?

- What new leaders might God have you invest in developing? Who comes to mind?

- What type of process can you envision for the leaders you're developing?

- What ministry environments can you make available to them?

- What relationships can you make available to them?

- How can you pray for those you are developing?

- Where might they need challenging? Where might they need support? How could you provide those things?

For further reading:

- *Leadership Coaching: The Disciplines, Skills, and Heart of a Christian Coach,* by Tony Stoltzfus

- *The Situational Leader,* by Dr. Paul Hersey

- *From Followers to Leaders,* by Robert E. Logan and Tara Miller

TEAM-BUILDING, PART 1

Building One Another Up

When I was leading a church staff, we went on retreat together once a month. The retreat was an overnight trip for two days. We did that for eight years—every month—and it was a sacred time. No one could schedule anything over it unless everyone on staff could make the change. Even when the church was small and we couldn't afford it, we found some free lodging and paid for the food out of our own pocket. It was that important. Why?

We'd start with half a day or even two-thirds of a day in sharing, relationship, and prayer. Then we'd have a one-word agenda: something like "assimilation" or "training" or "evangelism." Then we'd engage in a process of reflecting on that topic across all ministry areas: What's working? What's not working? What are we learning? What needs to change? What are the next steps? We weren't just conducting business; we were setting aside time to think strategically about a whole area that needed to be applied on a churchwide scale, and listening to God about where we needed to focus our attention.

The time helped us see and understand where we were going and why, and allowed everyone to contribute ideas, thoughts, and questions. And you'll notice we didn't skip over the relational element. We spent significant time on the front end deepening relationships with each other and with God.

Doing these retreats so regularly cost us a lot—in time, money, and energy—yet the times contributed so significantly to our teamwork and our understanding of each other that we all considered them well worth it. Why? Because relational elements like building trust, recognizing each other's strengths, and praying and learning together form the foundation of effective teamwork.

Consider all the good that could be done out of an environment of relational trust.

> **Relational elements like building trust, recognizing each other's strengths, and praying and learning together form the foundation of effective teamwork.**

A note from Colin:

Building relational trust takes time. It also involves being congruent—which means that our words, tone, and body language are all saying the same thing. We should also be highly sensitive to other people's opinions and even their worldview, with as little judgment about it as possible. If we respect differences we build trust. If we tell someone their view of the world is wrong or crazy, we break trust. We build relational trust by using the following broad behaviours:

- *Think of other people as being worthwhile, and value their diversity.*

- *Notice body language, breathing, personality style, tone, language, etc.*

- *Treat the other person with respect and integrity.*

- *Practice active listening at all times.*

- *Ask questions gently and sensitively, to show that you care about the other person.*

- *Avoid matching negative emotions.*

Therefore each of you must put off falsehood and speak truthfully to your neighbor, for we are all members of one body. "In your anger do not sin": Do not let the sun go down while you are still angry, and do not give the devil a foothold. Anyone who has been stealing must steal no longer, but must work, doing something useful with their own hands, that they may have something to share with those in need.

Do not let any unwholesome talk come out of your mouths, but only what is helpful for building others up according to their needs, that it may benefit those who listen. And do not grieve the Holy Spirit of God, with whom you were sealed for the day of redemption. Get rid of all bitterness, rage and anger, brawling and slander, along with every form of malice. Be kind and compassionate to one another, forgiving each other, just as in Christ God forgave you. Follow God's example, therefore, as dearly loved children (Eph. 4:25–5:1)

Doesn't that sound like an environment you'd like to be a part of? When people are part of a strong community founded in a common faith, they are more motivated to reach out in love and service to others. And isn't that what everyone wants for their ministry team?

This chapter—part 1 of teambuilding—focuses on the internal values of a team: things like sharing, relationships, prayer, and learning together. Through practices like these, you can develop a healthy working environment on your team. The following chapter—part 2—will focus on the external values of a team: the outward manifestation of practical service to others and effective ministry.

In this chapter, I am assuming that you already have selected the right people for your team (as discussed in chapter 3). Now we look at the skills you need to lead your team forward effectively, while building a solid foundation of teamwork and relationship.

Leading teams is a messy endeavor. In any group of people that spends enough time together—families, friends, coworkers, etc.—there will be challenges that arise. People don't always get along. They disagree. They want to go different directions. In some cases, it can get ugly. People begin gossiping, building alliances, shutting each other out, and attributing negative motivations to each other. You've probably been around churches long enough to know the same dynamics can occur in Christian communities.

So whatever group of people you are leading, you need to find healthy ways to work together—ways that build up and develop the members of your team so that you're prepared for maximum effectiveness. This chapter doesn't cover everything you might possibly need to know, but it does cover the basics for getting started so you can begin building a healthy team environment.

Here are some of the basic topics we'll address:

- Building trust
- Keeping clear relationships
- Getting people on board
- Recognizing accomplishments
- Learning together

Fair warning: It does take time to do this, but it's well worth the investment if you want to lead a team effectively. Don't go too utilitarian, trying to jump to getting things done while leaving out the relational and spiritual elements, especially in the early stages. Short cuts inevitably backfire and you'll end up doing more work in the long run.

Building trust

If there is no foundation of relational trust on the team, everything else will fall apart. That's true no matter how good you become at practicing the skills described in this chapter. Take the time now to build a foundation of trust. The most common error in building trust on your team is simply not taking the time necessary to do it.

> The most common error in building trust on your team is simply not taking the time necessary to do it.

Building trust means taking the time to get to know one another, creating relational bonds through conversation and shared experience. It means praying together and for one another. It means learning about each other's strengths and affirming them.

One very easy way to build in relational time is to take one of your team members out for lunch or coffee or breakfast, without any agenda. This is a pattern I used to engage in regularly when I oversaw a formal staff team. I would come in with no agenda and just relate to them as a person. I'd ask open-ended questions: How are you doing? How are your kids? The goal was simply to relate to them and their world on a personal level. They could talk about whatever they wanted to talk about. Some people would go very deep; others preferred just chatting. Open-ended questions would allow them to take the conversation wherever they wanted it to go.

A note from Colin:

Stephen Covey suggested that the first principle in becoming highly effective is to "Seek first to understand, then to be understood." This principle suggests that it is how we read and understand a person that is a key foundation to building a strong relationship. How do you get to understand someone? People want to know they are being heard. How many times have you heard yourself or others ask: "Do you know what I mean?" Real listening is rare.

An important point about these conversations: it's not about what you need as the team leader– it's about what they need. This can't be about your need to get deeply personal. It needs to be about their need to feel personally related to and cared for. It also requires that you'll need to share something about yourself at an appropriate level. Relationships are a two-way street. Consider whether you're willing to do that. If you're not, reflect on your reasons.

There is no substitute for time when you're not pressed. You can't force relationships, but you can intentionally create space for them to happen at times when you don't have your "supervisor hat" on. The most effective team leaders care deeply about their team members, and relate to them on a personal level. They also default to trusting their team members. That's not blind trust, simply an initial posture.

When I was a senior pastor and someone from the congregation came to me with a complaint or a criticism about one of my staff members, I didn't immediately assume that the person complaining was right. I had an initial default position of assuming the best about my staff members, knowing that sometimes complaints can be a result of misunderstandings. Secondly, I would ask, "Have you talked directly to the staff person about this?" If not, I would send them immediately to the staff person, so as not to triangulate.

I found that even in cases where there was legitimate cause for complaint, taking this initial posture helped immensely in resolving the issue. It was much more effective than assuming my staff member was at fault and rushing to blame them. This example illustrates both building trust with staff members, as well as the next topic: keeping clear relationships.

Here are some additional tips for developing trust:

- Connect with team members not only individually, but all together as a group. Both are important.

- Be sure to learn each team member's strengths and unique contributions—and call them out in front of others for those.

- Take time to listen well and ask questions.

- Pray with and for your team.

- Demonstrate vulnerability yourself at an appropriate level.

- Don't play favorites among your team members.

- Verbally express a commitment to each person's growth and continued development.

> **Be sure to learn each team member's strengths and unique contributions—and call them out in front of others for those.**

Keeping clear relationships

Once you have put forth the effort required to build an environment of trust, it becomes much easier to address conflicts as they arise. Keep short accounts. Forgive. Seek to understand. Bring in help from the outside if you need to. This is all basic conflict resolution advice... as well as basic discipleship behavior. Therefore, it is essential leadership behavior.

Be willing to admit when you're wrong. Remember that as the team leader, you set the example for everyone else. If they see you never being willing to admit you're wrong, they're likely to embrace that course for themselves too. Take the initiative even if you're only twenty-percent responsible for the problem and own your part. The value of leading by example is powerful.

A note from Colin:

This point is extremely important, but sometimes as leaders we get things wrong and others are aware of it but it is not brought to our attention. To offset this happening, create a culture of inviting feedback, where you ask people to help you grow as a person and leader. This also helps when you have to give feedback to others. When you get feedback:

- **Evaluate the whole message**—*If a person starts with something positive, the temptation is to stop listening after that.*

- **Listen, don't react**—*Seek first to understand.*

- **Treat it as important**—*It is if someone has raised it.*

- **Accept what is being said**—*Remember that accepting the feedback does not mean you agree with it, but you are willing to consider it.*

- **Be honest**—*We all get things wrong.*

Lead with kindness and an assumption of good will. Keeping clear relationships involves both honesty and kindness in the face of difficult situations. For example, when I had to talk with a staff person about an area of blatant weakness, I would begin with a posture of assuming that he was aware of it and willing to work on it. Even if that turns out not to be the case, you're beginning by giving them the benefit of the doubt.

Support accountability. Someone in a group I was a part of broke a confidence. Another party came up and shared something with me about it. It wasn't that what I had shared in the group was so horrible, but that the only way this other person could have known about it was through him. I needed to talk with that person to reestablish a clear relationship.

Be honest about struggles. I was once part of a staff where we were transitioning to the next level of organizational growth. God was challenging us to move forward, and as the rest of us made the jump to the next level of responsibility, one was unable to make that leap. He was a great guy and had been good at what he'd been required to do up to that point. But we had to be up front and clear about the challenges we were facing now, and how the rest of us had to carry an extra load if he could not do it. Our honesty led to a gracious transition for him, instead of an angry firing or a subtle undermining.

Talk about it. Once I had a person on my team who was more pastorally sensitive than I was. This is not an uncommon occurrence, but in this case he had a problem with my lack of shepherding ability. We also had some philosophical differences about who should be delivering pastoral care and how. But we had good communication and we talked it out. We never came to philosophical agreement, but we kept the air clear and were able to assume the best about each other's intentions.

Keeping clear relationships between yourself and everyone else on the team also positions you well when you need to step in to mediate conflicts or tensions that arise between other team members.

Getting people on board

Even if you as the team leader are quick and decisive, you need to take time to help your team members process things and unpack their thinking. It's not helpful to come down like you've heard from God on the mountain, announce where you want to go, and expect everyone to fall in line. By taking the time to process new directions and decisions with those you oversee, you'll not only have increased buy-in and ownership, but you'll arrive at clearer thinking yourself.

Here's one way I used to do this with my staff. When we made an appointment, I'd tell them, "When we get together, I'd like to talk with you about X." X could be what we were trying to accomplish, the best ways to go about something, or a possible change on the horizon. The staff members appreciated the heads-up and it allowed them to prethink the issue, so that when we got together they were prepared. Then I made sure to unpack their thinking first, asking clarifying questions to make sure I understood their perspective. I found that the staff members not only appreciated this approach, but it sharpened my own thinking as well.

Often we would isolate an issue or a question, then schedule a follow-up meeting for any further clarification or conversation that was necessary. Then we could make a tentative decision, and come back again to finalize our approach. Generally I found there was a "rule of three"—it would take three cuts at a problem to arrive at a solution. This meant I needed to make myself available to staff members, providing reasonable access and inviting questions and constructive criticism.

Taking the time to listen well, engage in two-way dialogue, and encourage feedback is more time-consuming, but yields vastly better results. People are committed to what they help develop. The best team leaders take that into account, communicating clearly, encouraging two-way dialogue, and allowing multiple passes at decisions.

In a later chapter, we'll address the topic of leading change. In many ways, that will be an expansion of this essential team-building skill. This type of dialogue, listening, and buy-in is precisely what's needed to bring about long-term change to the broader organization. But it starts right here with your team.

Recognizing accomplishments

Never go more than a month without recognizing and celebrating your team's accomplishments in some way. Most leaders underestimate how motivating this kind of recognition can be. People need regular affirmation for their hard work and the fruit of their labor. This is true both for the accomplishments of the team as a whole and for the accomplishments of particular individuals.

For the whole team, I use the example of a barn-raising. In farming communities, when someone needed a new barn put up—a job that was too big for just one person or one family—the whole community would pitch in. They came

> **People need regular affirmation for their hard work and the fruit of their labor.**

together, worked, cooked, and put up the barn in one day. Then that night, they had a meal and a dance in celebration of their labor. They came together, accomplished something big, and then celebrated as a community.

Teams are the same. Say your team pitched in and put together a great series of discussions and gatherings for new believers. Don't just immediately move on to the next thing. Take some time to congratulate the team and celebrate their accomplishments. Make it social and communal. You can call out individuals for particular contributions, but make sure it's clear to all that this was a team effort.

Here are some more tips on recognizing accomplishments:

- Serve as an encourager and maintain morale.
- Acknowledge peoples' accomplishments in front of others.
- Publicly support those who serve under you when they are criticized.
- Make sure all feedback is honest.
- Use teachable moments and specific examples.
- Create a job-review process, to stay current on accomplishments.
- Never reprimand in front of others.

Learning together

Even if you, as team leader, are aiming for cooperation and support, teams can easily become competitive environments: "Am I doing well enough?" "Am I doing better than so-and-so?" One way you can help combat that tendency is to create learning environments.

Learning environments are designed—of course—to teach people new things, but they are also designed to create a posture of humility. None of us know everything. All of us can learn from one another. There doesn't even need to be a lot of new content when we listen to one another's experiences. Just spending time praying together, listening for the voice of God, and asking him questions can help put people into a learning posture.

Set aside times to learn, pray, and listen together as a team. A volunteer worship team leader at a small church began setting aside times for team worship. She realized that the team was so focused on providing worship for the congregation that they weren't experiencing it together as a team. They began by asking God questions in prayer and listening for his voice. The experience brought about a new level of humility and learning on the team as they opened themselves to how God might want to develop them as worshippers, not just worship facilitators.

Every team needs some type of environment that involves learning, relationships, and trust. Even with many challenges, disagreements, and even fights over direction and theology, the team of apostles we see in the book of Acts went on to accomplish amazing things. One of the reasons for this was a baseline of trust and relationship. Even when there was sharp disagreement, they knew they were on the same team and ultimately wanted what God wanted. Only from that foundation were the apostles able to disperse throughout the known world, and among so many different kinds of people, the message of the gospel and a vision of redemption and unity. It was built on a foundation of trust and recognition that we are all part of the family of God.

Team Building Principles:

- Take time to be together regularly for extended periods.
- Affirm each member's unique contribution.
- Build in celebration times.
- Learn to ask for counsel from one another.
- Pray together; play together; plan together.

Prayer guide:

- As you pray through the individuals on your team, who is God bringing to mind? Why might that be?

- Of the topics covered in this chapter, which do you feel good about? Which do you feel you may need to work on?

- How might God use you to bring a sense of unity and purpose to your team?

- How can you pray specifically for those on your team?

- What action steps are you sensing God would have you take?

For further reading:

- *The Wisdom of Teams: Creating the High- Performance Organization,* by Jon R. Katzenbach and Douglas K. Smith

- *Leading the Team-Based Church: How Pastors and Church Staffs Can Grow Together into a Powerful Fellowship of Leaders*, by George Cladis

6

TEAM-BUILDING, PART 2

Spurring One Another On

A woman named Susan began an outreach to teen girls who became pregnant while still in high school. The idea came to her when she was volunteering at a food bank and saw a girl she recognized from church who was visibly pregnant. She wasn't sure what to say at first, but then reached out the girl.

"I learned that if a teen gets pregnant in the church she is most likely to leave the church because the church is not seen as supportive," Susan explained. "And if a teen gets pregnant and doesn't know Christ, she is not likely to turn to the church, because she thinks it is not for her." That needed to change.

Susan met with the principal of a local high school and began offering a four-week pilot program. It was well received, and the girls kept coming back. The connections led to relationships between Susan and the girls, and then grew to include some of Susan's adult friends—both churched and unchurched-- who also became role models and encouragers.

One significant need was child care, especially during school hours. Susan helped them get connected with a day-care center where the new moms took turns helping with all the kids, which freed them up during the school day to attend their other classes, college, and jobs.

Nine years later Susan and the team of volunteers are still running the program, now called Growing Pains (www.growingpainsprogram.org). They meet weekly at three locations—two high schools and a church—and offer classes on parenting, infant care, nutrition, first aid, budgeting, healthy relationships, etc. The moms (and the dads too) receive credits from their high schools for attending the classes. Not only are they learning parenting and life skills, but they are learning spiritual truths about God's unconditional love for them.

As the program has grown over the years—and some attendees along with it—it now encompasses parents ages sixteen to twenty-nine. They are single and married, churched and unchurched, and together with the team leaders and children there are about seventy-five people total, including attendance at all three sites. The parents many times say, "We are family."

Growing Pains is a great example of a missional team spurring one another on toward love and good deeds and truly making a difference as they come alongside one of the most vulnerable and underserved populations in their community. Their desire, which they are working toward collectively, is to create a safe and loving community where teen parents grow and experience the grace of God—a place to receive and offer help, encouragement, and support.

> And let us consider how we may spur one another on toward love and good deeds. Let us not give up meeting together, as some are in the habit of doing, but let us encourage one another—and all the more as you see the Day approaching (Heb. 10:24–25).

The end result of team dynamics built on a foundation of relational trust is effective outreach. A team that is strong internally will also be strong externally. That's just as true in personal discipleship for individuals. The inner life has outward expression.

Notice something important here: Often, team leadership approaches billing themselves as "results-oriented" begin with the outward workings of the team. What are we accomplishing? How can we accomplish more? Let's skip over all the *prolegomena* and get to what matters: results. I consider this approach short-sighted. Significant long-term results come from laying the relational and spiritual groundwork first, then moving forward to act out of that abundance. "First clean the inside of the cup and dish, and then the outside also will be clean" (Matt. 23:26). Fruits flow from roots. On teams, we can then spur one another on toward love and good deeds.

> Significant long-term results come from laying the relational and spiritual groundwork first, then moving forward to act out of that abundance.

The previous chapter focused on laying the groundwork of teambuilding; this chapter focuses on how to lead teams toward fruitful and effective ministry results. Here, we see the external values of a team: how a team shows its heart through love and good deeds toward the wider world. Here are some of the basic topics we'll address:

- Casting vision
- Clarifying direction
- Clarifying roles
- Clarifying strategy
- Delegating tasks and responsibilities
- Leading effective meetings

Casting vision

Much has been written about the importance of vision-casting. You likely already know that you need to cast a compelling vision for your team to work toward. You're aware that you need to paint a concrete picture of a desirable future that aligns with the kingdom of God. How will the world be different because of your work? What will that look like? It's like a jigsaw puzzle: The more clearly you can paint the picture on the box, the more clearly people can see how and where their particular piece fits into the puzzle as a whole.

> **A note from Colin:**
>
> *The why I talked about earlier in Simon Sinek's book is the fundamental purpose of a team or organisation. We need to sense why we are here (purpose) before we can know where we are going (a vision). Both of these, together, become the basis for all future actions.*

What's most often forgotten is how *often* you need to cast that vision. Even leaders lose vision in less than a month. One pastor, after receiving a compliment on his sermon, responded, "I feel like I pretty much say the same thing every week." And it was true— he consistently cast a vision for a new heaven and new earth, with a flourishing humanity contributing to that renewal. But it was compelling. Vision needs to be cast over and over in different words and in different ways— but the same vision.

As an exercise, read through Peter's speech at Pentecost in Acts 2. What elements of vision-casting do you see? What parts, even in the infancy of the church, function as reminders of what God has already been doing?

Often people need reminding more than they need teaching. The same is likely true of your team. They know why they are there—but they do need regular reminding of how compelling that vision really is.

Clarifying direction

Casting vision and getting people on board set the stage, but then it's time to get more specific about precisely what you are trying to get done. For example, say your church has a vision for getting more engaged with the surrounding community, as well as for compassion and service. That's great, but it could look dozens of different ways. What direction do you want to go with it? Tutoring neighborhood kids? Helping with refugee resettlement? Caring for the elderly with meals and companionship? You'll need to narrow your focus a bit if you're going to accomplish anything specific.

To a degree, your direction will depend on the opportunities in the community surrounding your ministry. Who has God placed in your path? Who has God placed on your heart? How has he equipped you to be able to help? Spend time as a team discerning God's voice. What direction is he leading? What could that look like?

One helpful exercise when embarking on a new direction is called "Achieve, Preserve, Avoid." Essentially, brainstorm answers to these questions:

- What do we want to achieve?
- What do we want to preserve?
- What do we want to avoid?

Answering these questions will help you get a better sense of the specific direction God is leading you. It moves you from clarifying your general direction into setting priorities and planning. You get a better sense of what the ministry will actually look like if it's successful.

Consider how the apostles planned as they expanded their ministry to bring the gospel to the Gentiles. They had to consider the culture of the people they were reaching, how it differed from their own, and then they had to answer these same questions. For example, circumcision: something to preserve or something to avoid? Jewish dietary laws? And then what about pagan Gentile practices—which of those could be kept as part of the culture, and which were incompatible with the basic message of Christianity?

> Together you will be able to hear from God and clarify specific direction much more effectively than you would alone.

Your team is an essential part of all of these kinds of discussions as it reaches out to surrounding communities. Together you will be able to hear from God and clarify specific direction much more effectively than you would alone.

Clarifying roles

Who is supposed to be doing what? This is the basic question of clarifying roles. On a team, each person will likely have different responsibilities. Each person needs to be very clear on their own responsibilities as well as those of the rest of the team members. In this way, your team can avoid duplicating tasks, letting tasks fall through the cracks, or just generally stepping on each other's toes because no one is clear on that first question: Who is supposed to be doing what?

Some ways to accomplish this clarity: Have written job descriptions. Compare those written job descriptions against day-to-day reality. Adjust when necessary. If you do make changes to team members' responsibilities, make sure to consult with everyone affected before making any decisions. (Changing people's job descriptions without talking with them first goes over very, very poorly.)

A note from Colin:

For this process to be effective, start by listing the existing roles. Then, conduct a systematic audit of the skills of the team, in order to understand how each individual can help the team reach its potential. A skill inventory should be done openly and constructively.

A team that doesn't have a clear understanding of roles, as well as a good grasp of the individual skills of the team, will inevitably be poorly aligned. Although this process can be tedious for some, it often helps reduce future frustrations. This is particularly important where the team is under pressure. In these circumstances, be sure that everyone understands all the team roles and skills—not just their own—to eliminate confusion or misunderstanding about who is doing what.

Have team conversations to lay out specific responsibilities, especially in gray areas. For example, if your kids' ministry is going to collect items and package them to give out to the homeless, is the children's director primarily overseeing that project, or is it the outreach coordinator? If it's a collaboration, be sure those two leaders are clear on which of them are to perform which functions.

Ideally, team members' responsibilities would align with their strengths. You wouldn't want someone who is not gifted organizationally being responsible for all Sunday morning setup or programming. There can certainly be stretch points and learning curves—and challenging your team members to grow is a good thing. Their roles should be a good fit with their strengths, allow opportunity for stretch and growth, and of course they should continue to grow personally outside of ministry.

However, in some cases, especially when teams are smaller and ministries are newer, people will need to function temporarily outside of their areas of giftedness. But that's the key word: temporarily. Recognize—out loud and in front of the whole team—that this person is sacrificing by working outside of his area of giftedness because of current needs. Then pray like crazy, both individually and as a team, that God would bring you the right person to fulfill that role in the longer term.

Clarifying strategy

Clarifying strategy addresses the question, *"How* are you going to work together?" Set aside specific time to think strategically and set priorities. As a team leader, you need to create the time and space to think strategically together with your team. Effective leadership is not just leading in isolation and then telling your team to implement your decisions. Processing strategy with them will help you lead much more effectively.

Delegating tasks and responsibilities

Delegation is an essential skill for developing your team members. Not only does it take work off your own to-do list, but it helps develop others. So why don't more leaders do it? The challenge is giving up control. If you don't do it yourself, how can you be sure someone else will do it correctly the first time? You also might need to let them do it differently than you would yourself. They might try and possibly fail. Giving up control is harder than it looks.

One of the reasons we sometimes don't want to release responsibilities to others is because we may not think they are as talented as we are. First of all, let's make the dubious assumption that's true. And then let's do the math. If we are a "100," but we're only able to give the area ten percent of our focus, that's a score of 10. But if we delegate it to someone who's only half as good—a 50—but they're able to give it eighty

> **Giving up control is harder than it looks.**

percent of their focus, that's a score of 40. Their overall score is four times better than ours, even if they're only half as good.

> *A note from Colin:*
>
> *Here are some more reasons that I have observed as to why leaders do not delegate.*
>
> - *Enjoying maintaining the impression of being overworked*
> - *Believing they are indispensable*
> - *Having a lack of trust in others*
> - *Having a fear of criticism by others*
> - *Having a fear of losing face*
> - *Being concerned at overloading other people*
>
> *Every leader needs a delegation process, and the following is one example of this:*
>
> - ***Identify the task/project**—Be able to explain it clearly, so someone can understand what is expected.*
> - ***Identify the right person**—Are they willing, capable, interested, and skilled?*
> - ***Brief the person and set goals and priorities**—The aim here is set specific goals, targets, and timing, and then to offer as much help in the form of support, as the task requires and as the person needs.*
> - ***Coach/support the individual appropriately**—The amount of support will vary according to the task, but in general it is better to be available to offer guidance than not, especially in the early stages.*
> - ***Recognise the effort or contribution**—It is important to jointly learn from the experience for next time and to offer thanks for the efforts, as well as recognition for a job done well.*

We sometimes don't want to release control because our standards are so high. But then we spread ourselves so thin that our quality level drops anyway. Give others a job they can really concentrate on, and they'll likely end up outperforming us. Plus, delegating gives them the opportunity to develop and grow.

There are two aspects of ministry that leaders need to be able to delegate. The first is tasks. These are specific, measurable jobs that need to be done. An example of a task is setting up twenty chairs. The person is told what to do. The second is responsibilities. An example of a responsibility is creating a prepared and welcoming environment for a class. The person is told what needs to be accomplished, and then she is responsible for finding a good strategy for making that happen: She has authority over decision-making.

By delegating not only tasks but also responsibilities, you develop your people to their fullest potential. Begin with tasks. Delegate a task to test faithfulness; see if the person follows through. If he does, you can give him an area to be responsible for and he can make decisions around how to accomplish that goal.

One thing I've found helpful is to appoint a leader who can then recruit and mobilize a team. The team then together can decide what needs to be done and be empowered to do it. That works far better than a committee getting together to make decisions about what others can and can't do and how they should go about doing it. It's much more empowering to entrust the leader and team with the responsibility and decision-making for the plan.

Of course, sometimes things will go in unexpected directions, which is part of the challenge of giving up control. A woman came to our church as an intern working in our children's ministry. She proved to be so helpful and valuable that we brought her on as director of children's ministry. She did an excellent job overseeing and running that whole ministry area, and I was very affirming and appreciative of the quality of the work she did.

I also noticed that she had really strong gifts in the area of pastoral care and shepherding, so I began to give her opportunities to do pastoral care work outside of the children's ministry area. Ultimately, we ended up changing her job description because she was even better suited in a pastoral role. Then instead of just having an excellent person handling the children's program and getting the work done, I now

> Developing people requires listening to the Holy Spirit, and being willing to change directions based on his leading.

had a staff person realizing her full potential—including her development of a new children's director.

This delegation of responsibility didn't go in the direction I intended, but it did go in a much better direction than if I had just had a specific job I wanted someone to fill. Developing people requires listening to the Holy Spirit, and being willing to change directions based on his leading.

Think of each of your team members individually. What strengths can you draw out and develop in each of them? What tasks might you delegate to that end? What responsibilities might you delegate to that end?

Delegation can mean a variety of different things. Be clear on which one you're asking for when you delegate. Which one you use will depend on the situation, the person you're delegating to, and their skill level.

1. Just do it; you don't need to report back.

2. Do it, and report back to me on how it went.

3. Do it regularly, and report back to me regularly.

4. Investigate and make recommendations to me, then we will decide together.

5. Gather data for me, and then I will decide.

Leading effective meetings

When it comes to meetings, less is more. Don't have meetings just to have meetings. When you are thinking of planning one, the first question to address is, "What are you trying to accomplish?" Is there something you want people to do? Is there a way you want them to feel? What do you want them to walk away with that they didn't have before the meeting? If the answer is something along the lines of disseminating information, you might accomplish that goal more effectively by sending out written information or recording a short video. Consider whether you really need a meeting or not to accomplish your goal.

Then, if you do, tailor that meeting to accomplish its desired ends:

- What decisions need to be made?

- What information do you need to present? What motivation do you need to tap into?

- What process do you need to lay out for people to follow?

- What do you need to do to keep that process on track?

- What next steps do you need to provide?

- Who might you need to pre-process before the meeting?

Often our meetings aren't very good because we're not clear on what we really want people to walk away with. If you know what results you want, you can know if you were successful or not. Consider what purpose you're trying to accomplish, and call a meeting with that specific agenda in mind, inviting only those who need to be there. For most purposes, not everyone needs to be in the room. And when people do need to be in the room, they'll know the meeting is relevant to them and their ministry.

A note from Colin:

Meetings are important, but many people see them as extremely boring, confusing, and a waste of time. In fact, most of us can tell stories about frustrating or annoying meetings we have had to endure. Ultimately, all meetings will be successful if the people involved feel that they have been of value. Here are some approaches that can increase the value of your meetings, if adopted and regularly practiced:

Purpose—Meetings should only be called where there is no other way to obtain the views or opinions of others in coming to a decision.

Preparation—Think about the goals that you want to achieve, and write them down.

Opening—Every single meeting should start and finish on time.

Control—Stay on track, and only deal with your goals for the meeting.

Close—Close the meeting strongly, outlining the actions that have been agreed upon.

Three other guidelines I'd highly recommend regarding meetings:

One, *everybody comes prepared.* When I had staff meetings, everyone was expected to come prepared for whatever the specific agenda was for that meeting. They were called on when it was their turn to present whatever they had prepared. I also used to have church board meetings where we had agreed that if any board members hadn't read the proposal in advance, they were not allowed to comment on the proposal or chime in with ideas. After we agreed on that rule—and enforced it when a man wanted to give his opinion anyway without having read it—preparation went up dramatically.

Two, *mark each agenda item clearly* about whether it is a matter for information, discussion, decision, or follow-up action. That way, people in the meeting know if they're just being informed of something as opposed to needing to make a decision about it. They also know if they have a takeaway assignment to go research something and report back about it. Review all assignments at the end of the meeting.

Three, *never do scheduling*. Handling scheduling issues—especially one-on-one scheduling issues—during group meetings is a big time-waster. Calendar coordination can generally be done more efficiently one-on-one, by email, or even with a scheduling/polling program like Doodle if there is a group involved. There's no reason for people to wait around while scheduling is being done.

Hopefully this chapter provides you with some practical ways to work together effectively as a team on mission. Much of the advice here revolves around clarity: knowing what you're doing and why. That's an example that has been set for us by our leaders since the earliest days of the church.

> In those days when the number of disciples was increasing, the Hellenistic Jews among them complained against the Hebraic Jews because their widows were being overlooked in the daily distribution of food. So the Twelve gathered all the disciples together and said, "It would not be right for us to neglect the ministry of the word of God in order to wait on tables. Brothers and sisters, choose seven men from among you who are known to be full of the Spirit and wisdom. We will turn this responsibility over to them and will give our attention to prayer and the ministry of the word."
>
> This proposal pleased the whole group. They chose Stephen, a man full of faith and of the Holy Spirit; also Philip, Procorus, Nicanor, Timon, Parmenas, and Nicolas from Antioch, a convert to Judaism. They presented these men to the apostles, who prayed and laid their hands on them.

So the word of God spread. The number of disciples in Jerusalem increased rapidly, and a large number of priests became obedient to the faith (Acts 6:1–7).

Prayer guide:

- As you read through the sections of this chapter, where do you sense God calling you to focus?
- What are some ways you might be able to remind your team of the vision and of their role in it?
- How can you pray for your team members?
- What action steps are you sensing God would have you take?

For further reading:

- *The Performance Factor: Unlocking the Secrets of Teamwork*, by Pat MacMillan
- *Death by Meeting: A Leadership Fable… about Solving the Most Painful Problem in Business*, by Patrick Lencioni
- *Spiritual Leadership: Moving People on to God's Agenda*, by Henry T. Blackaby and Richard Blackaby

DISCERNMENT AND FOCUS

Getting a Sense of Direction

A church I started used to meet on Sunday nights because that was the only time we could find space available. It was a terrible time for our community—people were focused on getting home and getting geared up for the week ahead. Eventually we found a space on Sunday morning, but it was only available from 8:30 am to 9:25 am, and we had to be out of the building completely by 9:40am. That seemed awfully early, but was preferable to Sunday nights. And again, it was the only thing we could find on Sunday mornings, so we took it.

But that's when we inexplicably started growing. We discovered we were reaching families with preschoolers. An 8:30 am service was late for them; many of those parents had been up since 5:30 am or 6 am. And the people volunteering in our children's ministry were excellent, so it caught on and those families stuck.

We also discovered that we were now the only Protestant church in town that allowed you to make your 10 am shift if you were waiting tables or working at the hospital. This insight led me to realize we had deliberately excluded people who might connect with God in church because their work schedule or lifestyle precluded it. We really did want doctors, nurses, police, and firefighters working on Sundays. These are essential services. We also want chefs and servers working so we can go out to brunch after the service—not so essential, but certainly nice. Plus, what about all the unchurched people who were busy on Sunday mornings? Maybe they had a car club or went camping for the weekends? We were basically telling them, "You may want to connect with God and church, but we don't have anything for you unless you are willing to do it in on Sunday mornings." Clearly, we weren't doing all we could to allow people to meet Jesus.

I held that tension in mind and a few years later, after continued growth at our Sunday morning services, we started a Friday night church. It was geared toward those who were recreational on weekends: campers, skiers, surfers, hikers. We placed an ad in the sports section of the newspaper: "Come to Friday night church and enjoy the rest of your weekend." Of course we were roundly criticized for this ad—by other Christians, not by non-Christians. The non-Christians loved it. But other Christians and other churches criticized us for not worshipping on the Sabbath and not keeping it holy. My response? "If worshipping on the Sabbath is the important thing, then that's sundown on Friday to sundown on Saturday. So at least in the winter, our church is technically more biblical than yours."

This chapter is about finding your sense of direction. It's about discernment, focus, and the leading of God. As I've read the Bible with this topic in mind, one of the things I notice is that many of the people featured in its pages spent considerable amounts of time wandering around or trying to figure out what direction they should be going: Moses wandering with his people through the wilderness; David hiding out in caves as he awaits the promised kingship; Abraham hearing the call of God and setting out to follow it; Jonah hearing the call of God and running in the other direction.

Most of the book of Acts traces the movements of various bands of apostles around Asia Minor and beyond. They didn't always know where to go. Sometimes there was a clear direction from God, sometimes it was a matter of preference or relationship, sometimes it was a desire to reach a certain group of people, sometimes it was the very practical matter of avoiding stoning and violence.

> Paul and his companions traveled throughout the region of Phrygia and Galatia, having been kept by the Holy Spirit from preaching the word in the province of Asia. When they came to the border of Mysia, they tried to enter Bithynia, but the Spirit of Jesus would not allow them to. So they passed by Mysia and went down to Troas. During the night Paul had a vision of a man of Macedonia standing and begging him, "Come over to Macedonia and help us." After Paul had seen the vision, we got ready at once to leave for Macedonia, concluding that God had called us to preach the gospel to them (Acts 16:6–10).

I wonder if it felt like playing a game of "hotter-colder" with God—where you have to just start moving in a direction and listening for either "hotter" or "colder" to see if you're going in the right direction, then, depending on geography, barriers, directions from the person in charge, and trial-and-error, you eventually figure out where you're supposed to be. I don't know if that's what it felt like for the apostles, but I certainly felt some of that when planting and leading a church. It was both a "listen for the voice of God" approach and a "figure it out as you go" approach. They worked together, and I firmly believe both are valid.

Sometimes our best plans were stumbled upon, as described above, when we were forced to make certain decisions due to barriers that later presented us with unforeseen opportunities. But that's not to say we weren't praying and listening to God. That's often how we recognized those opportunities—because we were paying attention.

Some leaders default to the planning side: They go through their checklist and do what they planned to do, only to find out that what they were doing wasn't what was needed. People weren't finding it helpful. Other leaders default to spontaneity: Don't plan at all, just stay open and something will happen. But sometimes it doesn't. Or sometimes, what happens isn't helpful.

What about a third way? I call it "fuzzy planning." It takes the best of both of those approaches and weaves them together. That's the cycle I try to follow: Listen for God, discern his voice, focus on a plan, take some next steps, then celebrate and recalibrate depending on where those steps have brought you. The road becomes clearer as you go, and you listen to God at each step along the way.

> ### A note from Colin:
>
> Franchising, whether it is done by a megachurch or a denomination, may have worked in the past but it is inappropriate in the twenty-first century. The sheer diversity of society forces us to try to understand the communities around us and compels us to apply biblical mission in a multitude of different ways. This is not an easy thing to do because we have never been here before. "Listening for the voice of God," becoming a student of your community, and "figuring it out as you go" may not feel comfortable, but welcome to the real world.

The road becomes clearer as you go, and you listen to God at each step along the way.

> Jesus gave them this answer: "Very truly I tell you, the Son can do nothing by himself; he can do only what he sees his Father doing, because whatever the Father does the Son also does (John 5:19).

As Henry Blackaby has suggested, "See where God is working and join him there." By listening to God and joining him in the work he is already doing in the world, we are letting God shape our values and vision. This is not just a chapter on strategic planning—that is, where we decide on a goal and then come up with the most efficient way to get there. It's more about prayerful exploration to discern how God may want to use us and our ministry.

In this chapter, I'll address subjects like vision, goals, prioritization, and planning, and I'll do my best to give solid, practical advice. At the same time, don't forget that each of these topics is subject to discernment and listening for the voice of God. That means they are unlikely to take you in a straight line from A to B. There's likely some wandering around involved. As you listen and discern and try again, your path will take shape.

Important questions to ask

Nearly every book on leadership talks about the importance of knowing your values, vision and mission. In ministry I've always dealt with these three items, but I've discovered that adding purpose and approach can be extremely helpful as well.

- Values answer the question, "What is important to you?"

- Purpose answers the question, "Why do you do what you do?"

- Vision answers the question, "What is your preferred picture of the future?"

- Mission answers the question, "What do you want to accomplish?"

- Approach answers the question, "How do we want to accomplish this?"

There's a good reason for thinking through these areas: You can't know whether you're successful unless you know what you're trying to accomplish. You probably can't know in advance exactly what you want your ministry to look like in ten years, but setting some target to move toward will help you move forward in a productive direction.

Although I've been in ministry for forty years, I revisit the question of values, vision, and mission regularly—most recently just this past summer. I find it helps to sharpen my thinking in these areas periodically. Here's what I, with the help of my team, came up with for my organization, Logan Leadership:

> *Our Values*: Empowerment of others, outward-focused ministry, a posture of ongoing learning, adherence to the Great Commission, and multiplication.
>
> *Our Purpose and Vision*: We align with the heart of the Father in our desire to see every person living, growing, and multiplying together as disciples of Jesus who demonstrate the kingdom of God among all peoples.
>
> *Our Mission*: We believe that our calling is in catalyzing leaders to accelerate their movement toward this vision.
>
> *Our Approach*: By combining biblical principles with social science insights, we help leaders sharpen thinking skills, focus strategic actions, contextualize solutions, and create reproducible processes, increasing their ministry capacity.

I'm proud of this work, as it helps me and the others on my team get clear and remain focused on what we are really all about.

Try this with your team or group: Think through your ministry together and complete the boxes below. Don't short-circuit the process by doing it yourself instead of thinking it through alongside others; you'll have missed out on some significant opportunities for team-building, motivation, and getting people on board to go in the same direction—not to mention that your results won't be nearly as good.

ROBERT E. LOGAN | LOGANLEADERSHIP.COM

Values: What is important to you?

Purpose: Why do you do what you do?

Vision: What is your preferred picture of the future?

Mission: What do you want to accomplish?

Approach: How do you want to accomplish this?

Discernment

Once you have thought through these areas, it's time to return again to prayer and discernment. What did you hear God saying to you through this process? What seems important? What opportunities do you see? Where do you already see God working? What is already going on in the community where God has placed you? Who is already there? How can you help?

Take time in prayer, both alone and together with your team. Spend time getting to know the surrounding community. Don't be in a hurry. Listen for God's voice.

Brainstorm possible initiatives

In any situation, there are dozens and dozens of possible initiatives. Start brainstorming. List a whole bunch of potential actions, both large and small. What are the possibilities? There are likely many more than you can think of. But when you have a long list, start grouping the ideas and prioritizing them. What seems important? What seems doable? What seems most strategic?

Setting goals and prioritizing

Next comes the time for setting goals. Let's say you believe you've heard God's voice challenging your new but growing church to become more multiracial. That's a good long-term goal, from which you could generate many possible more specific short-term goals to take you in that direction. For instance, initiatives you may have brainstormed could include partnering with the local public school or participating in a panel discussion on race and faith. Depending on where you are, you may not be on the panel but might be in more of a listening position.

After listening to the Holy Spirit, setting a goal, and brainstorming to multiply options, you and your team will need to set priorities. You likely have limited time and energy and aren't able to carry out every good idea, so you'll need to focus on just one or two for now.

Also recognize that you may not meet all of your goals. Even good goals, faithfully pursued, are not always successful. Consider how the apostle Paul set goals to visit faraway lands to bring the gospel. He planned to go to Spain (Rom. 15), but we have no clear historical record of him having made that visit. He also deeply desired to go to Rome to preach the gospel (Acts 19). We know he did get there, but not under the circumstances he probably initially had in mind—as a prisoner under guard rather than as a free man (Acts 28).

Sometimes we accomplish our goals and sometimes we don't. But having them gives us direction and focus for our work. Discerning, brainstorming, and prioritizing allows us to focus our energy more productively.

A note from Colin:

The biggest problem I find when working in this area is that leaders believe intent is a goal. The diagram below illustrates the goal's transition from a mere desire, or intent, into a clear, focused outcome. From its beginning as a vague concept, or "fluffy" aspiration, a goal is challenged with "what" and "how" questions. The answers form an eventual framework for specific actions.

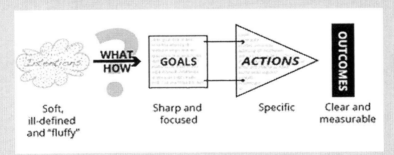

A helpful way to develop sharp goals is to imagine a future time when the goal has been accomplished. Ask yourself the following:

- *What has been achieved?*

- *How does it feel?*

- *What am I thinking?*

- *What are others saying?*

Once you have completed this process, work backward to think about what steps you need to take between now and then. Ask yourself "What should I do now to achieve my goal?" On their own, goals are poor motivators. However, breaking them down into single, achievable and incremental steps will support and inspire every individual to stick to the task.

Sometimes we accomplish our goals and sometimes we don't. But having them gives us direction and focus for our work.

Planning and implementing

With specific initiatives in mind, work out concrete plans for accomplishing them. If your church has decided to focus its energy on partnering with a local school, how could it go about doing that? Which school? Who could you talk with at the school to determine their needs and openness to partnering? When and how should that partnering be done? Which people from your church should be involved? What is a realistic start date, and what preparation needs to be done?

Planning takes us into the detail work. Some leaders enjoy this stage and others don't. If you don't, make sure you involve other gifted people from your team who do. They will notice things you won't and will ask the questions you overlook.

Sometimes the vision is clear but you need the plan to be sharpened as you go. You can be moving in a strategic direction, but have the flexibility to adapt and shift as you get closer. In some cases, leaders may be tempted to overplan—to wait to get started until every last detail is mapped out. But that approach usually results in inertia, and we need to be in motion in order to discern the next steps. We are living in a world where we don't—and can't—know everything in advance. But if God wants us to do something, he has given us enough to get started.

So take the first steps. Talk to people. See what others are doing. Ask how you can join them. For example, if you have a connection with a local school official, you may want to schedule a conversation before you have all the details of the plan figured out. That conversation is likely to help you on the way.

You don't need to know everything in order to move forward, but you do need to have a few next steps so you can begin moving. The apostles modeled this approach for us as well. They didn't know all the details ahead of time—because no one can—but they did listen to God, plan what they could, and then got started.

Adjusting as you go

It's a maxim—and a true one—that nothing ever goes as planned. The only guarantee is that something unexpected will happen. What that means is that as you implement your plan and move forward, you will need to pause periodically to take stock of where you are and listen for the voice of God. Then you'll need to make whatever adjustments are needed as you go.

When I was a pastor, I charted weekly attendance of adults, youth, and children at our Sunday services and kids' programs. As a data geek, I even plotted year-to-date averages. Historically, our children's attendance would rise at the same rate as our adult attendance. Then for four months, I noticed that our adult attendance was continuing to grow, but our children's attendance had remained flat. That was a shift in the usual pattern, so I dug into the data to try to figure out what was going on.

I discovered that we were having trouble sustaining the number of children's workers needed for our current programs. We'd recruit more, but then have turnover. After talking with some people, it sounded like our children's workers were getting tired. We were expecting them to serve every week without a break. That's more often than I was preaching. Plus, there was no natural end point to the job; you worked until you burned out, then quit.

What we decided to do was to give the entire children's ministry the summer off. We recruited a whole team of separate people just for the summer, and changed the program to make it less staff-intensive. We called it "summer spectacular," and we had games and activity centers. I was surprised by the volunteers we got: college students home for the summer and school teachers who had the summer off. These were people who loved kids, but after working with them all week didn't also want to do it on Sundays. They were more than happy to volunteer once a week over the summer, though.

In the fall, the regular children's workers came back with renewed energy and focus. They had really appreciated the summer off, and we decided to give them every summer off. Not only did it help significantly with burnout and retention of children's workers, but it underscored the importance of sabbaticals, breaks, and rest. We also had the benefit of developing two pools of workers. Many of the summer teachers knew they'd be off again in the fall, so were willing to volunteer multiple summers. I had never realized we had people who would prefer summer-only ministry opportunities.

The principle is to pay attention to trends and shifts, dig deeper to understand why they are happening, then make strategic adjustments based on that information. You have to adjust as you go based on progress so far. It's like the cycle I guide people through in coaching relationships: action, reflection, renewed action, reflection, etc.

Creating a planning rhythm

You might be thinking that all of this clarifying of vision, setting of goals, planning, reflecting, and making adjustments takes a lot of time. True. But if you want to accomplish your goals effectively, it takes far less time than just trying to muddle through.

So plan ahead. Set aside time for a regular planning rhythm. Do whatever works for you. Below is the planning rhythm I used when I was a senior pastor leading a staff team. I found it helpful for focusing on both long-range and short-range planning. Plus, by setting aside regular times on my calendar in advance, I made sure the planning rhythm actually happened.

- Once a year, I set aside a week to think and pray through the coming year.

- Once a quarter, I set aside a day to think through the next three months.

- Once a month, I set aside three or four hours to focus what needs to get accomplished in the next month.

- Once a week, I set aside an hour for specific calendaring and action planning.

The plan itself is nothing. Planning as a process is everything. The plan itself will likely start changing as soon as you begin implementing it. But planning as a process helps you engage with God and others as you reflect on what God is doing. It helps you be intentional and proactive about what you are doing with your time and energy. Start small, experiment, refine, build on what

> **The plan itself is nothing. Planning as a process is everything.**

you're learning, move to the next logical piece, and see how the clarity increases as you move forward.

A man named Steve was serving as a superintendent for his organization coordinating the building of medical facilities and bringing medical teams to Ethiopia. The Ethiopian government was very happy with the work, as it included both quality and frequency and was much needed. However, one high-ranking government official told him, "We really do appreciate all the work you've been doing, but you're overlooking an urgent need." Steve asked what that might be. The official said, "Reforestation."

The government official went on to explain how radical deforestation in the region had recently resulted in catastrophic flooding along the Udo Escarpment, leaving several villages destroyed and eleven villagers dead. The official further explained how deforestation diminished subsistence farming and was therefore a major cause of extreme poverty. As he saw it, extreme poverty caused by deforestation was the root problem. Medical problems—often resulting from extreme poverty—could be considered a symptom.

Steve had a business degree; he hired a seedling nursery manager and started Eden Reforestation Projects, which promotes employment for villagers who grow, plant, and guard trees to maturity in developing countries. The combination of employment and forest restoration breaks the cycle of poverty and environmental damage.

Granted, this was a far different opportunity from what Steve had planned and been working on, but he saw that it had the potential to be an even better one. The plan itself is nothing. Planning as a process is everything. Sometimes the adjustment we need to take guide us in new directions we cannot yet see.

Prayer guide

- What are some ways you listen to God for direction? How have you heard from him in the past?

- Who could help you sift through your values, purpose, vision, mission, and approach?

- Who else could you invite into your planning process?

- What might an action-reflection-action cycle look like for you? Give a specific example.

- How does God need to change you to help you become more effective in discernment and focus? What steps might you take in that direction?

For further reading:

- *Pursuing God's Will Together: A Discernment Practice for Leadership Groups*, by Ruth Haley Barton

- *Advanced Strategic Planning: A 21st-Century Model for Church and Ministry Leaders*, by Aubrey Malphurs

- *The Leader's Journey: Accepting the Call to Personal and Congregational Transformation*, by R. Robert Creech and Jim Herrington

LEADING CHANGE

Herding Cats and Other Feats of Patience

I had planted our church with a commitment to church planting from the very beginning. It was a part of our DNA. However, as the church was growing and God was blessing it, our pastoral team had the sense that we weren't just meant to plant a few churches here and there—that the vision God wanted us to have was way bigger. I do recognize that founding pastors have a lot more influence than pastors that take on an existing congregation, but I knew that for a vision this big I was going to need *a lot* of buy-in and ownership. So we engaged in a major strategic planning process.

We began with an all-church survey taken during the actual worship service. We took five to ten minutes from the service to have people fill it out. Then I made a list of all the opinion leaders in the church—the people who other people listened to. They were leaders in matters of public opinion, and influenced the opinions of others whether or not they had any official leadership role. I found that there were about sixty opinion leaders—about ten percent of the adult portion of the congregation. (As an aside, I've found that in most congregations, the percentage of opinion leaders holds steadily at about ten percent of the total.

So whether or not your church is formally organized according to small groups, it still really *is* organized according to small groups.)

I decided to break these opinion leaders down into five groups of twelve people each, and have them over to our house for five consecutive weeks for an interactive dinner to talk about church planting. As far as these opinion leaders knew, they were a randomly selected cross-section of the church, but they were key people who were in touch with the rest of the people in the congregation so they would be accurate representatives. I sent out five questions in advance for people to think about and told them I'd just be listening. We'd serve chili and cornbread, and I'd just ask the questions and listen to people's thoughts. Here were the questions:

- What are our strengths? What do we do well as a church?

- What are our weaknesses? What are your concerns?

- What church needs do you think we should address in the next two to three years?

- What community needs do you think we should address in the next two to three years?

- What obstacles need to be addressed before we begin our strategy to start new churches?[1]

I then decided to do something that sounds horrible. I knew, looking at this list of sixty opinion leaders, that some were more negative and outspokenly critical than others. I decided to put the twelve most negative people all in the same group, instead of sprinkling them throughout the groups. (I do not recommend trying this at home. I know many congregations have more vehemently negative obstructionists than I was dealing with in this case. You could be eaten alive.) Most of my people in the church were generally in alignment, since church planting had been

---

1   Notice that I didn't ask if we should start new churches, but what obstacles need to be addressed before we do. The idea was to get all the concerns and questions and doubts out there.

part of the DNA from the beginning. However, as a nod to self-preservation, I didn't book my group of naysayers first. I saved them for last.

A note from Colin:

*In any process that may involve ideas outside of the paradigm of individuals, it is wise to work with the **distribution curve of responses**, and use this to introduce new thinking. The following flow of responses is a helpful one.*

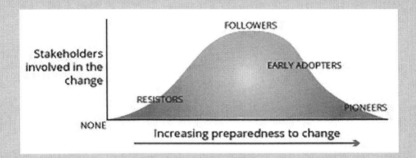

If you are trying to introduce a new idea, don't start with everyone—each person's preparednees to change is very different. Start with the pioneers who are usually quick to adopt, and allow them to talk to the early adopters, who talk to the followers, who talk to the resistors (who probably won't buy in anyway!).

The first four groups sailed by. I sat listening and taking notes, writing down everything they said. Then the fifth group came to my house. One guy began by pulling out a legal-sized sheet of paper filled out on both sides with his objections. After he started, others chimed in. It was a feeding frenzy, as if someone had dropped bloody red meat into the ocean and the sharks started coming for it. Several times I had to say, "Wait, I need to be sure I'm getting this all down," as I was scrambling to keep up. We spent forty-five minutes on just the last question, listing problems, concerns, issues, and objections. It was a rich, rich brainstorming experience.

I thanked them all for coming, then looked over and prayed over that list. I asked God, "What do these folks not understand about you and your ways that would lead to these concerns and fears?" That group was so helpful to me. It helped discern and inform the themes of my preaching schedule for the next two years. When I saw a fear, I'd look for a biblical character who shared that fear or demonstrated the opposite. I began to understand the principle of "praying in the opposite spirit": If you're running into a scarcity mentality, you focus on generosity—or being willing to lose your life rather than hanging onto it. What was also incredibly helpful was that the other people shared some of those same concerns and fears, but were too loyal and supportive to say so. The upcoming sermons applied to everyone.

After the interaction dinners, we had a weekend board and staff retreat to pray through and process the vision for planting and the feedback we had received. We discerned together where God wanted us to go, and put together a draft of a three-to-five-year plan. Then to test that plan, we hosted a series of cookouts—bring your grills, bring something to grill, and give your feedback on the draft of the plan. We scheduled three cookouts with forty people each, and ended up needing to schedule a fourth one. Based on what we heard, we made some revisions, clarified some things, and addressed some of the issues people had.

Next we had all-church dinners, where we presented our plan and rolled out our goals for church planting. We transformed the auditorium to look international and global, with flags and foods from all different nations. We shared our vision and announced our big church planting goal—and even then, asked for feedback via a response card.

After all of that, we only had one family decide to leave our church because of not being on board with church planting. Their exact words: "We just don't believe that the church should be that focused on reaching unchurched people." They had processed through the whole thing and thought about it, and they just didn't agree with the direction. I gave them referrals to three other churches in the area that believed as they did, and they joined one of those. They were happy and the church loved them—it was a great match.

It was a long, long process, and I'm not even including all the individual one-on-one meetings I had. These were just the big efforts toward getting buy-in and ownership. We went overboard to involve people in the process, because we knew they'd only be on board with something they'd helped to develop.

Leading organization-wide change is one of the most daunting tasks of a leader. I generally included a relevant Scripture passage toward the beginning of each chapter in this book, as a way of showing how the Bible addresses the topic at hand. In this case, we're going to look at the Jerusalem Council in Acts 15.

First of all, this council was a big deal. The question of circumcision and adherence to the law of Moses for Gentile believers was a hot-button issue of the day. It was controversial, and many good people disagreed about what direction to go. It was far from a foregone conclusion what would be decided. The issue was not a slam-dunk, but a thorny matter of people's identity, culture and values. These things are not easily changed. Read through the passage now, with an eye toward how they handled the process:

Certain people came down from Judea to Antioch and were teaching the believers: "Unless you are circumcised, according to the custom taught by Moses, you cannot be saved." This brought Paul and Barnabas into sharp dispute and debate with them. So Paul and Barnabas were appointed, along with some other believers, to go up to Jerusalem to see the apostles and elders about this question. The church sent them on their way, and as they traveled through Phoenicia and Samaria, they told how the Gentiles had been converted. This news made all the believers very glad. When they came to Jerusalem, they were welcomed by the church and the apostles and elders, to whom they reported everything God had done through them.

Then some of the believers who belonged to the party of the Pharisees stood up and said, "The Gentiles must be circumcised and required to keep the law of Moses."

The apostles and elders met to consider this question. After much discussion, Peter got up and addressed them: "Brothers, you know that some time ago God made a choice among you that the Gentiles might hear from my lips the message of the gospel and believe. God, who knows the heart, showed that he accepted them by giving the Holy Spirit to them, just as he did to us. He did not discriminate between us and them, for he purified their hearts by faith. Now then, why do you try to test God by putting on the necks of Gentiles a yoke that neither we nor our ancestors have been able to bear? No! We believe it is through the grace of our Lord Jesus that we are saved, just as they are."

The whole assembly became silent as they listened to Barnabas and Paul telling about the signs and wonders God had done among the Gentiles through them. When they finished, James spoke up. "Brothers," he said, "listen to me. Simon has described to us how God first intervened to choose a people for his name from the Gentiles. The words of the prophets are in agreement with this, as it is written:

*"'After this I will return
 and rebuild David's fallen tent.
Its ruins I will rebuild,
 and I will restore it,*

ROBERT E. LOGAN I LOGANLEADERSHIP.COM

that the rest of mankind may seek the Lord,
 even all the Gentiles who bear my name,
says the Lord, who does these things'—
things known from long ago.

"It is my judgment, therefore, that we should not make it difficult for the Gentiles who are turning to God. Instead we should write to them, telling them to abstain from food polluted by idols, from sexual immorality, from the meat of strangled animals and from blood. For the law of Moses has been preached in every city from the earliest times and is read in the synagogues on every Sabbath."

Then the apostles and elders, with the whole church, decided to choose some of their own men and send them to Antioch with Paul and Barnabas. They chose Judas (called Barsabbas) and Silas, men who were leaders among the believers. With them they sent the following letter:

The apostles and elders, your brothers,

To the Gentile believers in Antioch, Syria and Cilicia:

Greetings.

We have heard that some went out from us without our authorization and disturbed you, troubling your minds by what they said. So we all agreed to choose some men and send them to you with our dear friends Barnabas and Paul— men who have risked their lives for the name of our Lord Jesus Christ. Therefore we are sending Judas and Silas to confirm by word of mouth what we are writing. It seemed good to the Holy Spirit and to us not to burden you with anything beyond the following requirements: You are to abstain from food sacrificed to idols, from blood, from the meat of strangled animals and from sexual immorality. You will do well to avoid these things.

Farewell.

So the men were sent off and went down to Antioch, where they gathered the church together and delivered the letter. The people read it and were glad for its encouraging message (Acts 15:1–31).

As you read through the passage, what did you notice? Here are few of the highlights that stood out to me:

- **Verse 2:** A variety of people were appointed to represent the people and engage in conversation.

- **Verse 3:** They began by focusing on the positive: The only reason they were even discussing the matter was because so many Gentiles had come to faith in Jesus. It was a problem of how to handle the growth and increasing diversity of the church—a good thing, but one that brought with it questions.

- **Verse 6:** "They met to consider the question" implies coming to the table with an open mind, even about a controversial subject.

- **Verse 7:** Much time was devoted to discussion, which likely included listening to multiple voices from different perspectives.

- **Verse 23:** When the matter had been decided, they agreed upon an implementation plan and a way to communicate that decision.

Now if you have read some of the rest of the New Testament, particularly the letters of Paul, you'll know that the issue of circumcision and adherence to the law of Moses was not forever put to rest by the decision of this council. Paul continues to address and clarify the matter in his letters and elsewhere in Acts, sometimes correcting the teachings of others. Real and lasting change doesn't happen quickly.

However, this council was an important early step toward leading change. A disagreement arose, and a process was put into place to address the matter. It was a thoughtful process, one that allowed for the expression of multiple and varying perspectives to be voiced. Many people were included.

That's a significant lesson for the leaders of today's church: You need to involve people in the planning process and incorporate their feedback in order to gain ownership for change. Sooner rather than later, you'll need to prepare people to embrace what's next. That means helping them become part of the change process. Passive acquiescence isn't what you're going for. You've got to be people on board with full ownership.

> **Change is not optional in ministry—it's a given. Things will change: circumstances, demographics, culture. The question is how we respond.**

Change is not optional in ministry—it's a given. Things will change: circumstances, demographics, culture. The question is how we respond to external change and how we go about promoting positive change. Therefore, one absolutely essential skill leaders must have is the ability to orchestrate change effectively. That includes anticipating change, planning for change, helping others to handle it well, and steering the process to a positive outcome.

If all of that sounds challenging, you're right. No one said this would be easy. If you have heard anyone actually say that it *is* easy, you can rest assured that they're lying and/or have had no real experience in actual ministry contexts.

What I have included in the rest of these chapters are essentials that you'll need to focus on, and put time and effort into. These are not magic bullets. They are not "five easy steps." They are not guarantees. We're talking about people here—and getting a group of people to move in a new direction is one of the hardest callings of a leader.

Yet these are the areas to focus on if you want to have a fighting chance of success in leading change:

- Don't be in a hurry
- Cast the vision
- Consider how you will free up time and energy
- Think through who you will need to work with
- Process people
- Incorporate feedback
- Strengthen relationships throughout the process

Don't be in a hurry

Change doesn't happen overnight. It's difficult, and if you imply otherwise you're underestimating the challenge of real change. Even small changes are disruptive. Think of challenges of jetlag, or even a couple of time zones—and that's a minor, temporary change.

Don't be in a hurry. Leading change well takes months or years, depending on the scope of the change and on how much influence you have in your current role. Give people plenty of time to process and prepare for change. It probably took you a while to come up with the ideas for change; give others the same courtesy of time. Often leaders forget that they had plenty of time to come up with the ideas for change, ask questions, and get used to it. The people in the congregation haven't had that same lead time. To them, this is all new and they're naturally not sure what to think about it.

> ## *A note from Colin:*
>
> *Change is the process of moving from the end of the old to the beginning of the new. Most leaders I have worked with get that, but forget about the period in the middle of these two. William Bridges calls this the neutral zone—that in-between state is so full of uncertainty and confusion that simply coping with it takes most of people's energy. The neutral zone is uncomfortable, so people are driven to get out of it. Some people try to rush ahead into some (often any) new situation, while others try to back-pedal and retreat into the past.*
>
> *Rosabeth Moss Kanter, Harvard Business School professor and author, says that change is hardest in the middle. Everything looks like a failure in the middle. Everyone loves inspiring beginnings and happy endings; it is the middles that involve hard work. As grand promises give way to the tough challenges of implementation, there comes a point when even true believers have doubts.*

Cast the vision

John Kotter is a change expert, and he outlines certain reasons change doesn't happen. The number-one reason is a lack of a sense of urgency; if you're satisfied with the status quo, there is no reason to change. Why go through the pain of changing if you're content with the way things are? There needs to be a certain level of dissatisfaction with the present situation to provide the motivation to move forward into something unknown. Because change is hard, people need a pretty good reason to do it.

The other condition needed for change to be successful is a vision of a preferred future. People need to be able to see that there could be something better. Without that—even if there is significant discomfort with the status quo—change won't happen.

People need a direction. They need to be able to see where they'd like to be and believe it's a possibility. Otherwise, why try?

To me, one of the best pictures of vision in the Bible is Moses looking out over the Promised Land from Mount Nebo (Deut. 34). They've come from slavery in Egypt and wandering in the wilderness. There is significant discontent with the status quo. There is also somewhere to go. We may not be there yet, but there is a promised land, and together we will get there. It may take a long time, it may be difficult, but we will overcome adversity and we will get there. Seeing the vision of what could be and casting it for others, modeled by Moses for the Israelites, is rooted in living by faith. It's about seeing what God has called us to do and doing it—even when there is a long road to be traveled.

And in Moses' case there was definitely a long road. Taking a direct route from Egypt to the Promised Land would have been a journey, but not a forty-year journey. Moses and the Israelites, however, taking an indirect and even circular route with many stops along the way, managed to stretch it to a forty-year journey through the wilderness.

The wilderness wanderings are not a bad metaphor for leading change: Barriers, problems, complaining people, nostalgia for a past of bondage, and even outright rebellion. Even if you know precisely where you want to go, the actual getting there with a large group of people is much harder than it looks and takes a lot longer. (Basically, the larger the group, the longer change will take. Changing direction for a small group will not take as long as changing direction for a congregation, which will not take as long as changing direction for a denomination. But the same basic principles apply to all ministry settings.)

> **Vision-casting is about seeing what God has called us to do and doing it— even when there is a long road to be traveled.**

People also require constant reminding about where they're going and why. Most of us, even leaders, can lose vision in less than a month. Effective vision-casting must be repeated, intentional, and take many different forms. In the day-to-day business of life and leadership, it's incredibly easy to lose sight of where you're going. Strong leaders keep sight of their long-term direction and communicate it effectively to others.

Here are a few common strategies for how leaders go about repeated vision-casting. Consider how some of these methods could be applied to your ministry context.

- Focused prayer

- Personal example

- Rewards and recognition

- Powerful stories

- Sowing seeds by sharing small ideas

- Appeals to scripture

> **God continues to prepare us for a future that we don't yet fully see.**

God continues to prepare us for a future that we don't yet fully see. His work is not done. We are even now being prepared for change—and a future we cannot truly comprehend.

Consider how you will free up time and energy

Change requires a lot of us. How will you free up the time and the energy you need to focus and move forward? If you're looking at making a change of any significance, you won't be able to do it in the margins. You'll need to free up time and energy to focus on it. Consider: What can you put off? What can you delegate? What can you stop doing all together? There are many different ways to free up time, so start with these "three Ds": delay, delegate, delete.

Consider also what changes you may need to make to prepare the way. Sometimes even for congregation-wide change, you may need to make a change in your life personally. If you want your church to become more outwardly focused, what are you doing to be more outwardly focused yourself? You might need to change what you're doing and some of your own personal habits.

> *A note from Colin:*
>
> *As part of preparing the way, spend some time around the question: What resources do we need as part of this change (time, materials, equipment, money, etc.)? People need to know that the leaders of the change process are serious, and prepared to commit themselves and the appropriate level of resources required to implement the change.*

If you are not willing to make personal changes, or make changes that will free up your time, consider how motivated you really are to do what it takes to lead the change you have in mind. You won't be able to lead others where you're not willing to go yourself.

Think through who you will need to work with

Another reason John Kotter cites for change not happening is the lack of a guiding coalition. If you're looking at organizational change in any significant capacity, odds are you can't pull it off alone. You're going to need to work alongside others.

Consider who those others may be. First there are coworkers: key people to work alongside you to facilitate the change process. Second are influencers: people who are widely connected to others who would need to embrace the vision. Consider who has relational influence in your circle—they will need to be included in the discussion and planning process. Third are gatekeepers: the people who will either provide or deny permission for moving

LEADING CHANGE

forward with change. Fourth, and finally, are the impacted: people who will be affected, either directly or indirectly, by these changes. An example of this group would be parents, when you are making changes to a children's ministry.

Identifying the people you'll need to work with to facilitate change is the first step. From there, you can think through actions and strategies to communicate well with people, so they can more readily embrace the change.

Processing people

If the people merely *consent* to the vision, they're essentially promising not to block you. If they have *ownership* of the vision, they want it to happen as much as you do, and they're willing to invest of their time, money, and talents. There's a big difference.

Get ownership by processing people. You'll need to dialogue with various stakeholders, listening and asking for their ideas and questions. Even if the pastor or board still makes the final decision, processing people well will help you avoid a lot of potholes.

People are committed to what they help develop; involve them in the process. Include people in early discussions, considering possible objections, brainstorming, and assignment. Be sure to do all of this before the decision is made, not afterward. It's at least twice as hard to bring people on board to accepting a decision that has already been made.

Also be sure to separate the discussion from the decision. Never present an idea and expect to make a decision on it in the same meeting. Give people time to process it and come up with ideas and concerns after they've had time to reflect.

In some cases, this will require you to have a meeting before the meeting... and a meeting after the meeting. Every meeting is really three meetings: the meeting before the meeting, the meeting itself, then the meeting after the meeting. Talk with people one on one, give them time to process, get support before bringing the idea to a formal meeting, and then process people again after that meeting to see what they are thinking.

Unless you help people process enough to the point where they actually buy in and feel ownership over the change, they won't help implement it. Just getting the preferred decision handed down doesn't mean people will embrace a new reality in their hearts. Try some of these strategies to help your people process potential or upcoming changes:

- Sow seeds: Get input before making decisions.
- Involve people in the planning process, so that they are more committed.
- Meet with key influencers before the main meeting to hear them out.
- Create space for people to share ideas and concerns before decisions are made.
- Use focus groups to hear what God is putting on people's hearts.
- Create times for listening prayer.

Incorporate feedback

If you process people well, you will get feedback—a lot of it. Be sure to do something with that feedback you have asked for. If you ask for people's thoughts, and then completely disregard all of them, you'll soon find yourself with a credibility gap.

People like to see their fingerprints on the final plan. As an added bonus, including different perspectives almost always makes for a stronger plan all around. People may have provided you with some truly valuable ideas for moving forward; don't waste them just because you didn't think of them yourself. People are committed to what they help develop, and they are more likely to be willing to commit to a well-thought-out plan that reflects their own input.

When the plan is announced, those who were included in the dialogue feel that they knew about it beforehand and they can often see the impact of their own concerns or questions reflected in the overall plan. They might not like everything, but they're more likely to think, "I can see how they came to that conclusion, and I can see the impact my input had."

Incorporating feedback well creates an environment of being heard and feeling listened to—and a much greater chance of ownership and success in moving forward.

When you have incorporated people's feedback into a workable plan, try it out on a smaller scale first. You don't have to change everything at once. Try just one small change first. Or, just make a change in one ministry area and see how it goes—or just gather a small group of the willing and try something out. I call these pilot projects. Start small, evaluate, adjust, reevaluate, and try it again. Once it's working well, you can expand the initiative and others will be more likely to get on board as well.

Strengthen relationships throughout the process

People always need relational support, but especially so in times of change. This isn't a time to neglect pastoral care, but to increase it. Times of change call for extra-intentional relationship building. Take the time now to strengthen relationships as you process change. Many leaders do the opposite—and feel the consequences.

A sample change process

Let's take children's ministry. Say you have decided that some changes need to take place in children's ministry. The easy way would be to write down the changes you think should be made, and then send out an edict. That would also be an extremely ineffective way to move toward change. You might create more resistance than cooperation. You need to get your team on board.

First, create a "task force" to involve others in the solution process. Ask for input from those currently leading and serving in the children's ministry, as well as creative thinkers and teachers in the congregation. Include insight from parents and children in the program, as they provide valuable perspective. Each of these groups are stakeholders — people who have a vested interest in the solution — and should be involved.

Then listen. What are you hearing from the parents? From the teachers? What are you hearing from God? What are you trying to achieve through these changes? Maybe you are hearing that you want to develop more compassion in the children. What are some ways you might be able to do that? Ask for input. Have some focus groups and listen to ideas. Research some nonprofit organizations in your area. Take a "vision trip," to find out what others in the community are doing. How might you be a part of what God is already doing?

After listening, the task force can draft a plan. Possibly they decide to partner with a community organization that allows children to participate as volunteers. After all, why reinvent the wheel? You can send out volunteers without creating any extra overhead. Write out what that might look like and process it with key stakeholders: "Here's what we are sensing from God. What's missing?" Listen carefully to what they say, make changes, and revise the plan. When you finalize the plan, you'll likely have broad agreement and support behind it.

In leading change, you'll find that the process is everything. Avoid the temptation to short-circuit it.

Planning Guide for Leading Change

The following is a sample planning guide you can use to implement change in your ministry context. Use these questions wisely to bring about a preferred future for the group, team or church you're leading. You can customize it to your ministry context by answering the following questions. Take some time to think through each one and answer them thoroughly; these are the seven most important questions to consider when leading change. You'll be amazed at what God may do over time.

1. How will you free up time and energy to focus on the change process?

2. Who are the key people who can work with you to facilitate the change process?

3. Who are the key influencers who need to embrace the vision and/or be included in the discussion and planning process?

4. What permissions need to be secured? From whom?

5. Who are the people/groups most affected by the proposed changes? What impact will each face?

6. What can you do to help people embrace the change?

7. How will you strengthen relationships during the change process?

A change process led well

One pastor leading a church that was in a turnaround situation invested the necessary time to lead change well. It was not a fast process. It has taken six years so far. For the first few years, it seemed like nothing was changing, but the pastor was building trust, making small but significant changes to create an outward focus, and naturally transitioning over some of the lay leadership. Slowly but surely, the church began to look outward.

Now in the last year and a half, the church has gone from being mainly white retired people to also including younger families and some new believers from an Iranian Muslim background. (Twelve of them have been baptized so far.) They also have started a Hispanic congregation. Over time, with slow and strategic changes, the Holy Spirit can shape and change things with a steady influence.

What would probably have happened, if this pastor had gone in the first month and announced all the changes to current programs and structure that allowed the congregation to become a more welcoming and inclusive place for younger people and for people from a different culture? Odds are, it would have been a nonstarter and wouldn't have worked at all. If by some miracle it had worked, almost all of the original members of the congregation would have left. The pastor would still have had a church, but it likely would have been nondiverse in a different way. As it was, the original members of the church felt heard, cared for, and included in the decision-making process. During the first four years, not one left the church. Almost all of them are still there six years later.

That's a change process led well.

A note from Colin:

Leadership plays an important role in the success of change. This leadership needs to be clear, strong, and congruent from the outset.

- **Clear:** *It is almost impossible to lead change if you do not stay as close as possible to the action. During change, it is not a good idea to delegate the key elements.*

- **Strong:** *Change is never a place for the fainthearted. Once started, people will look for direction from their leaders to allay their concerns.*

- **Congruent:** *The words of a leader must be matched by deeds. Leadership must be entirely committed and consistent at every step. Leaders must engage directly with individuals and teams, and listen to feedback and make adjustments when necessary.*

Prayer guide

- What changes are you hoping to see on the horizon in your ministry?

- How have you communicated the vision for change so far?

- What additional ideas have you picked up from this chapter that might be helpful to try?

- What are you hearing from God, as you contemplate ways to bring change that respect the people who he has already placed in your ministry?

- With whom do you need to talk?

- What other steps are you sensing God would have you take?

For further reading:

- *Building the Bridge as You Walk on It: A Guide for Leading Change*, by Robert E. Quinn

- *Leading Change*, by John P. Kotter

- *Start with Why: How Great Leaders Inspire Everyone to Take Action*, by Simon Sinek

COMMUNICATION SKILLS

It Takes Three Cuts to Get It Right

Early on in my church, we launched a membership class. It was designed to be a way to get people on the same page and moving forward together. It was a really good class—in my opinion—but we observed that people were often taking about eighteen to twenty-four months of hanging around the church before they took the membership class. We asked around and discovered that because of the name "membership class," people had to basically pre-decide that they wanted to become members before they took that class. By that time, they hardly needed the class. They had already figured out our vision, values, etc., just by hanging around for a long time.

So we tried another cut. This time we called it the pastor's class. That helped a lot with assimilation. We changed some things to make it more focused on getting people plugged in. Then one time I met a new family after the service. They were super-excited about the church, just bubbling over with enthusiasm. I asked, "Have you taken our pastor's class yet?" The man was surprised by the question. "Why should I do that? I don't want to become a pastor."

So we restructured—and renamed—the class again. This time we carefully called it by a name that reflected who it was designed for: the newcomers class. We thought through more carefully what newcomers want and need. They want to meet the pastor, meet other new people, get connected, hear about the direction of the church, grow spiritually, and get educated about how they can become a part of the community. To that end, we put a greater emphasis not only on getting people plugged in and connected, but did some significant teaching on spiritual gifts and made a direct connection to joining small groups after the eight-week newcomer's class finished.

It took quite a bit of time, but on the third cut we got it right. After that, ninety percent of people who finished the newcomer's class got into a small group, and ninety percent began using their gifts in a ministry of some kind. Good communication—to and among your people—takes at least three cuts to get right.

> **Good communication takes at least three cuts to get right.**

There is an important spiritual aspect to healthy communication. Like all leadership skills, it first needs to be built on a foundation of discipleship. A leader needs to live a life of obedience in areas such as making and keeping promises, avoiding gossip, not lashing out in anger, and practicing patience in listening. Only from such a foundation can more precise and strategic leadership communication skills be built.

James writes about this essential discipleship bedrock of communication skills:

> *My dear brothers and sisters, take note of this: Everyone should be quick to listen, slow to speak and slow to become angry, because human anger does not produce the righteousness that God desires. Therefore, get rid of all moral filth and the evil that is so prevalent and humbly accept the word planted in you, which can save you.*

Do not merely listen to the word, and so deceive yourselves. Do what it says. Anyone who listens to the word but does not do what it says is like someone who looks at his face in a mirror and, after looking at himself, goes away and immediately forgets what he looks like. But whoever looks intently into the perfect law that gives freedom, and continues in it—not forgetting what they have heard, but doing it—they will be blessed in what they do.

Those who consider themselves religious and yet do not keep a tight rein on their tongues deceive themselves, and their religion is worthless. Religion that God our Father accepts as pure and faultless is this: to look after orphans and widows in their distress and to keep oneself from being polluted by the world (James 1:19–27).

Listening well, being honest, and keeping control over one's tongue are essentials for leaders. From there, leaders can build more specific skills, such as learning to communicate new information to key people before communicating it to the congregation at large. Specific communication skills and strategies are built on the foundation of spiritual obedience. Both must be in place for effective leadership communication. Below are some of the topics we'll be covering in this chapter:

- Listening well

- Asking good questions

- Providing feedback

- Emotional intelligence

- Adapting to work with different kinds of people

- Resolving conflict

To be effective in ministry, you need to be able to communicate well with others, including those who are different from you. It's also essential for leaders to learn skills like listening well, asking good questions, and resolving conflict.

Listening well

Too many people go about leading without listening first. They dive in, doing what they think needs to be done, without really knowing if they're hitting a point of real need or not and without knowing if what they're doing is truly effective. As Carl George has said, "Help is not help unless it is perceived to be helpful."

Listening—indispensable for true ministry—is both a practice and a skill. It is a practice in the sense that you must intentionally set about doing it. It is a skill in the sense that you can continually study its dynamics and learn to do it better. How do we practice listening and hone our skills?

Here's who we need to listen to, in order to serve well:

1. The people we want to serve: They are the people best positioned to tell us about their needs, hopes, fears, and desires. We need to know them.

2. Other leaders who are already serving in this area: Don't start from scratch when others have already been serving here. Find out what they have already learned.

3. The Holy Spirit: There is someone who knows the needs of people more intimately than those who serve or those who receive service. Practice listening prayer.

Only once we have listened can we truly serve. However, note that I mean real listening, not selective listening. Too often, leaders are simply listening for what they want to hear. One time I was overseeing a church planter who was starting a new church in the beach communities of southern California. He was absolutely convinced that what was needed to reach the unchurched people in that area was a traditional worship service with hymns—everything old-style and traditional.

I was familiar enough with that area to know that was not their typical musical motif, so I asked him to go out and do a survey of the people in that community. He came back saying he discovered that they wanted traditional music. I'm not sure who he talked to, what his methodology was, or if he even conducted the survey. His church plant later failed, and I wonder if in part it was due to selective listening—he heard what he was listening for. If you're really not open to learning or doing anything differently based on the data you get, then it's better not to ask the questions at all.

> **A note from Colin:**
>
> It is important to recognise that in familiar situations, we often hear what we expect to hear. Listening as an active process involves:
>
> - being motivated and wanting to listen
>
> - paying attention, being aware and interested in understanding
>
> - sharing responsibility for communication with the speaker
>
> - using learned listening and hearing skills

Listening is hard work. It may look like you're doing nothing, but it requires focus and concentration on someone other than yourself. Good listening allows you to put yourself in someone else's shoes—even when that person may have a very different perspective from your own.

Self-focus is the enemy of good listening. As a ministry leader, take note of self-focused thoughts that arise in a given day: *How are others seeing me? Am I respected? Do I have influence? Am I seen as successful? How do I compare with other ministry leaders?* Self-focus (also known as pride) makes listening well almost impossible. We cannot prepare our own statements at the same time as we listen to others. One of them must give. Self-focus is something we need to give up in order to have the mental space necessary to truly listen to what others have to say.

Too many leaders think leading means talking rather than listening. Listening is viewed as passive or weak. On the contrary, it's one of the most effective tools of leadership there is. Before you can lead people, you need to listen to them. You need to find out what they need, what they think, what motivates them. You need to understand them. Only listening will accomplish that goal.

> **Self-focus makes listening well almost impossible.**

Here are some key practices for listening:

- **Listen with openness to the Holy Spirit**: To be good listeners, we need to be centered in the Holy Spirit—not coming in with an agenda, but really open and seeking to listen to God's voice. This is the case both when we are alone and when we are listening to others and helping them hear God's voice—no preconceived agenda, but openness to what God may want to do.

- **Listen with focused attention**: We need to set aside time to listen with our full, focused attention. We can do this by minimizing distractions, both internal and external. Focused listening is hard work and requires practice and intentionality.

- **Listen with patience:** Good listening requires longer than we expect. Be willing to go the extra mile to really be sure you are understanding the other person—even when it takes a long time.

- **Summarize what you are hearing without evaluating:** When we have listened, we should try repeating back to the person what we hear them saying. That way we can check to see if we are hearing them accurately. As much as possible, try to summarize what you are hearing objectively, not making judgments or evaluations.

- **Invite people to say more:** When people stop talking doesn't mean we stop listening. Rather, we should invite them to say more. Often doing this will yield important additional information or insight. It often communicates that you are truly interested in listening to their perspective.

- **Listen for understanding:** As you listen, seek mutual understanding. Try to make sure you are on the same page as the other person, that you are hearing what they are saying and understanding it as they intend it. Make sure you're not just assuming you know what they said, but that they are feeling accurately heard.

- **As you listen, seek insight:** Pay attention to insights and discoveries as you listen. Look for those "ah-ha" moments. Sometimes the person talking will not notice them unless you underscore what you are hearing. The goal of listening is understanding and insight.

Scripture speaks to the great value of listening:

Let the wise listen and add to their learning,
and let the discerning get guidance (Prov. 1:5).

To answer before listening—
that is folly and shame (Prov. 18:13).

Asking good questions

The corollary skill to listening is asking good questions. Asking the right questions can yield you a wealth of insight and perspective.

> **A good question is one that makes people think—one that makes them stop in their tracks to consider their response. A good question doesn't have an easy or obvious answer.**

A good question is one that makes people think—one that makes them stop in their tracks to consider their response. A good question doesn't have an easy or obvious answer.

Consider questions others have asked you that made you stop in your tracks to reflect. What came of those experiences?

Now consider how you ask questions. How many of your questions are yes-or-no questions? How many have strictly factual answers? How many have obvious or rhetorical answers that you're leading the person around to? What are some truly good questions you have asked others?

The value of asking good questions lies in getting people to reflect and think creatively. Good questions open up possibilities people may not have thought of otherwise. They also allow people to come to their own conclusions rather than be told what the answer is by others. Asking good questions draws people out, helps them feel heard, allows you to gain insights, and opens up new avenues you may not have thought of. It's an essential leadership tool no matter what your particular role.

Good questions:

- **Are open-ended**: Make sure none of your questions can be answered with yes, no, or just one word. Good questions make people think through more thorough responses. They are not designed to lead people down a predecided path, but as a process of discovery to help them gain insight. For instance, instead of asking, "Have you reached out to everyone concerned?" try asking, "Who else might you reach out to?"

- **Have a significant purpose:** We ask questions to raise awareness, to increase expectation of God working, and to focus responsibility. Consider how different types of questions could contribute to each of these ends.

- **Explore interconnected issues:** Often through asking questions, we can help people see connections between different areas that they may not have thought of as related. "What does X have to do with Y? How might X and Y be related?"

- **Highlight options:** Good questions raise multiple options. They don't box people in, but expand their possibilities. Use questions to encourage brainstorming and creative thinking about potential solutions.

- **Move people toward action:** Good questions lead to real-life steps. They take people from rehearsing a story to reflecting on that story, to moving into a course of action.

Pay attention to the questions you ask during the course of these next couple of days. Learn to ask good questions, and notice how much more powerful and creative the answers become.

Providing feedback

Although listening and asking questions are the most essential communication skills, it's also true that good communication must go two ways. It includes the ability to speak clearly. Reciprocal communication is the ability to clearly transmit your message, and to take other people's responses into consideration. It looks at how clearly individuals communicate, as well as the value they place on feedback.

If we think about it, God has established prayer as a reciprocal form of communication. We are to pray and ask. We are to pray and listen. And God, for his part, both speaks and listens. God, as the ultimate effective leader, listens to his people and empathizes with them:

> The LORD said, "I have indeed seen the misery of my people in Egypt. I have heard them crying out because of their slave drivers, and I am concerned about their suffering. So I have come down to rescue them from the hand of the Egyptians and to bring them up out of that land into a good and spacious land, a land flowing with milk and honey—the home of the Canaanites, Hittites, Amorites, Perizzites, Hivites and Jebusites (Exod. 3:7–8).

Likewise, effective communication between people goes both ways. We speak and we listen. Only by communicating clearly to those we lead, and by listening to their concerns, can we lead well. Healthy communication—for God, for leaders, and for all of us—is reciprocal communication.

Here are some key principles for communicating clearly and providing feedback:

- **Never start with feedback.** That's a major misstep. Take plenty of time to listen and ask questions first—otherwise your feedback will not be based on much of substance. Only give feedback when it's absolutely needed, and never tell someone something that you can get them to come up with on their own.

- **Make sure you have permission.** Consider who has invited you to speak into their life. Who might want you to serve as a sounding board for them? If you're unsure, ask. It's always better to ask first than to dispense unwanted feedback. I very regularly preface any comments I make by saying, "I have some thoughts on that. Would it be okay if I shared them with you?"

- **Start with affirmation.** Even when your main feedback might be a critique or a suggested change in direction, always begin with some type of affirmation. State what you agree with and what they're doing well. Positive reinforcement should far outweigh any type of negative feedback.

- **Give feedback gently** rather than in a "here's what to do" manner. Try stems like, "I wonder about... ," "From my experience I've found... ," "It seems like you're missing a key point here... ," or even, "I think if you proceed in this direction you may be making a mistake. . . ."

- **Close the loop.** Feedback is very easy to mishear or misunderstand. Close the loop by asking, "What did you hear me say?" How the person phrases it back to you will tell you a great deal about what they're hearing and feeling and how they might be interpreting your feedback. Don't leave that up to chance.

Emotional intelligence

The most effective leaders possess emotional intelligence. This includes things like insight, being able to see what another person may be thinking, good interpersonal skills, and the ability to calm your emotions rather than letting them control you.

Unsurprisingly, leaders need at least a basic level of emotional intelligence in order to lead others effectively. Emotional intelligence means our capacity to recognize, understand and harness our own feelings and the feelings of others. It draws on two simple concepts. To be "intelligent" or "applying knowledge appropriately," and also to be "emotionally astute" or "aware of feelings and applying them appropriately."

A note from Colin:

An emotionally intelligent individual has the capacity to talk about feelings and to accept feedback, to discuss their emotional reactions, and look for opportunities to gain new perspectives. Such people also have a high sense of self-worth, do not take themselves seriously, and are even relatively lighthearted and easygoing in their character. They also:

- *Avoid making decisions that create inner values turmoil*
- *Have a firm grasp of their capabilities*
- *Continually assess themselves realistically*
- *Are comfortable talking about their limitations and strengths*
- *Engage in having a laugh at themselves*
- *Are open to continual learning*

In the ministry of Jesus, we see emotional intelligence at every turn. Jesus listened and asked good questions. He displayed keen insight into motivations and feelings. Remember his conversation

ROBERT E. LOGAN | LOGANLEADERSHIP.COM

with Nicodemus (John 3)? With the woman at the well (John 4)? With Bartimaeus the blind man (Mark 5)? With the Pharisees, as he refused to become defensive or engage in fruitless debates (Luke 20)?

Consider the many ways Jesus demonstrated emotional intelligence in these conversations and others. We're seeing a lot more than knowledge, correctness, and statements of fact. We're seeing depth of insight and an understanding of human nature.

Other leaders throughout the Bible have echoed this emotional intelligence in their leadership. Nehemiah's actions demonstrate depth of emotion, patience, intentional action, and the ability to handle conflict effectively. On the other hand, King Saul failed in these same areas—to his great detriment.

Maturity—not just of the mind but of the heart—is a key for effective leadership throughout the Scriptures. Read some books on the topic of emotional intelligence, talk with a mentor or therapist about it, or get an online assessment to see where you're currently at. Although emotional intelligence is famously difficult to measure, it's absolutely essential for Christian leaders, and therefore well worth learning more about.

Adapting to work with different kinds of people

I worked with a lot of different kinds of people when I was planting a church, and later while leading a staff. I work with a lot of different kinds of people today as I coach across multiple denominational groups, in different parts of the country, and even internationally. With one client of mine, even with just an hour-long session once a month, I mentally set aside the first ten minutes of the session for catching up and small talk. It's important to this man for developing and maintaining rapport. If I were to dive right into business, he'd likely feel slighted personally. With another client, we exchange brief greetings, and then she dives right into whatever her primary concern is for that session. She would feel I was not making the best use of the time she is paying me for if we were to make small talk for ten minutes.

They need, want, and expect different things. That's the point of this section: Treat different people differently. Not everyone wants the same thing. Some people are naturally more relational; some are naturally more task-oriented. Some are fine with processing ideas aloud, just to see how they might sound; others hear such musings as a plan they must implement. Some people need to see the big picture before they can understand how all the details fit in; others need details in order to be able to see the big picture.

I find using the DiSC profile, which allows you to see how different people function differently in work and team environments, to be an incredibly helpful tool to adapting my own style to better suit the needs of the person I'm talking with. It helps me see through their eyes and begin to understand what's most important to them.

> **A note from Colin:**
>
> The DiSC profile is based on "different doesn't equal wrong, different equals different." To understand others, we need to know ourselves as well as know others. Unfortunately, we have a propensity to start a connection by judging—we see in others what we are looking for. If we are to move on, we need to follow these steps: Understand, Respect, Appreciate, Value.

In this way, adapting to different working styles is similar to working crossculturally. You can use the same principles. Since we are called to reach not only people like ourselves, but everyone, we must cross barriers. Sometimes those are cultural barriers, as when the apostles were sent to the Gentiles—to "Judea and Samaria and the ends of the earth." Doing that is difficult because we often don't know what to do, aren't sure what the "rules" are, don't speak the language (either literally or culturally), and/or fear rejection.

It's a scary thing for most of us to cross to the other side of the street. It's uncomfortable. We don't want to treat others as completely foreign from ourselves—after all, they are people too, also made in the image of God. But we also don't want to gloss over real differences that we need to understand and respect. We will certainly make mistakes, but the important thing is to risk, to try, and to be open to learning.

Yet even within our own culture and within our own congregations, we need to be able to see through other people's eyes in order to reach them and serve them well. Consider someone in your own family, even a spouse. Even if they're not of a different culture, chances are you have a hard time understanding their point of view sometimes. We

> It's good for us to stretch our minds and try to see through other people's eyes.

need to be able to put ourselves in someone else's shoes and understand what matters to them and how they think.

This effort not only helps us love others well, but it helps us not become calcified into our own views and perspectives—becoming inflexible like the Pharisees. It's good for us to stretch our minds and try to see through other people's eyes.

Often we can learn a great deal: a posture of servanthood, and how to communicate respect and value to those who think differently. In fact, if you want to run a healthy team—as referenced in earlier chapters—you absolutely need to be able to work with, and communicate with, people who think quite differently than you do. You need that "detail person" who annoys you with minor questions (minor from your perspective). You need that cautious person who raises concerns about potential barriers and pitfalls. You need the person that presses you forward and wants you to move ahead.

Resolving conflict

Part of being a leader is having the hard conversations. That means caring enough to engage in the difficult issues rather than avoiding them. That means talking about the things that are controversial—where emotions run high and relationships can become strained. We'll need to dialogue with those who don't necessarily agree with us about topics that really matter.

It is easier, and tempting, to avoid these kinds of conversations all together. But to move forward effectively, we will need to address certain things—maybe not everything, but some difficult conversations will be necessary. How do we negotiate those conversations with respect? With openness? With honesty?

Sometimes that can take the form of correcting or challenging others with an eye toward their betterment. It's clearly a fine line to walk to know when to confront and when not to, but sometimes confrontation—done in love—is warranted.

Yet we often forget that addressing conflicts and difficult situations also means courage and vulnerability. It means saying the hard, honest things about our own life, even when we may feel afraid. Leading with vulnerability can encourage others to be honest as well, paving the way for a culture that goes beneath the surface and allows people to really know one another and address the differences that exist.

A note from Colin:

Conflict is often perceived as being negative, destructive, and undesirable. People go to great lengths to avoid it, even when they acknowledge that it exists. We often deny or gloss over conflict, under the misconception that conflict of any kind is a bad thing. However, conflict is a natural part of our lives.

Individuals and groups within families, organisations, societies, and countries have values, needs, feelings and resources that differ from others. These differences inevitably lead to conflict. Conflict in itself is not problematic. However, it can be destructive if it isn't successfully channeled and resolved. If handled properly, conflict can highlight problems that need to be rectified, lead to new ideas and behaviours, enhance communication, and foster better long-term relationships between individuals and groups.

Here are some key principles for addressing conflicts and difficulties:

- **Look to the Scriptures for guidance**. Consider some of the many conflicts people in Scripture dealt with and how they handled them, whether well or poorly. Matthew 18 is just the tip of the iceberg.

- **Identify the real issues.** Given your ministry situation, what issues might need to be addressed? Are there relational tensions on the team? Are there theological divisions? Are there challenges that leave your team discouraged? Those matters can often be helped by respectful, honest, and loving dialogue.

- **Look at your own motives.** There are a lot of wrong ways to go about having difficult conversations. First take a step back and look at your own motives. Do you have an axe to grind with someone? Do you feel the need to be proven right? Do you want to win? Be willing to be honest about your own shortcomings. Share when you have been wrong or convicted. Be the one to go first in this, even if others have done wrong.

- **Start one-on-one.** If you have a conflict with someone else, go to them individually without involving others. Avoid gossip at all costs. See if you can reconcile the issue by just talking between the two of you.

- **Involve others only when necessary**. Try to ensure that whoever else becomes involved can be impartial and helpful. Ideally, they could be leaders in the church.

- **Generating and evaluating options.** Together, try to generate some possible options and solutions. Try to see if you can come to some agreement that addresses everyone's concerns and interests. If you cannot come to resolution, see if there is a way you can "agree to disagree," so that you can continue to live in peace.

- **Pray every step of the way.** Pray first, pray during, pray after. When possible, pray with others. Prayer will help us rely on God every step of the way.

Few leadership skills are more important than good communication skills. They can be the difference between a ministry being healthy and accomplishing its mission or going down in flames and crisis. Communication skills are related to almost every other chapter of this book. You'll need them in order to cast vision, to gather and lead your team, to develop your leaders, and to empower others. Investing in developing better communication skills now—wherever you already are—will yield significant dividends in ministry down the road.

> **Communication skills can be the difference between a ministry being healthy and accomplishing its mission or going down in flames and crisis.**

Prayer guide

- How do you need God's help in developing your communications skills?

- Where are your strengths? Where do you need to improve?

- What feedback have you gotten from others about your communication skills interpersonally? How does that play out in your ministry?

- Who are the people in your ministry that you have the most difficulty communicating with? How do you need to grow personally?

- What steps do you think God may want you to take as you grow in this area? What people or resources has he already given you?

For further reading:

- *Talk Like TED: The 9 Public-Speaking Secrets of the World's Top Minds*, by Carmine Gallo

- *Fierce Conversations: Achieving Success at Work and in Life One Conversation at a Time*, by Susan Scott

- *A Failure of Nerve: Leadership in the Age of the Quick Fix*, by Edwin H. Friedman

10

ADVANCED PEOPLE DEVELOPMENT

Working with Key Leaders

Effie approached me one Sunday after a membership class I taught. She was a young woman in her early twenties, married with two young children, and our church was quite small at the time. She told me how much she had enjoyed the class. Effie then proceeded to tell me what types of compassion ministries our church needed in order to provide outlets for those gifts: a ministry to bring food to people when they are sick or have new babies, hospital visits, a crisis hotline, etc. She listed every social need under the sun. "We don't offer any of that at this church!" she exclaimed. Unsurprisingly, her spiritual gifts test results—received during the class—indicated mercy and leadership.

How would you have responded? My first inclination was defensiveness: "Of course we don't have all that! We're a small church just getting started. What did you expect?" Fortunately, that first response was only internal. I thought for a few minutes and—recognizing the leadership impulse and the vision she clearly had—said, "You're absolutely right. How can you be part of the solution?" My desire was to take the energy she had and move it forward positively by empowering her to the degree that she was able. Had

I mishandled that response, she could easily have become a critic. (See the earlier section in this book on leading change.)

Instead, I empowered Effie to develop this ministry area, and met with her regularly to debrief her ministry planning and help her grow personally. The first thing she did was start praying. She soon began to recognize the resource shortages she was facing. A ministry of the scope she envisioned would require a good deal of coordination and communication. She was a visionary leader, but she would need an organizer if she was going to pull this off. She recruited Judy, a woman in the church with the gift of administration, and Judy created a system for organizing and rotating volunteers and for communicating needs when they arose. Together, they launched a ministry called the Care Team.

Effie soon realized she would need at least ten volunteers to avoid having the same few people always making meals and getting burned out. As she recruited people in the church to join the Care Team, she passed their names on to Judy, who plugged them into the system. However, as Effie talked to potential volunteers, she saw that buying the extra groceries would be a stretch for some. Others wanted to serve and give, but felt that their cooking skills were insufficient. Both money and culinary skills were resources necessary to the success of this ministry. Through pairing people together, she was able to spread the load and fill in those resource gaps. Some people even made it into a social occasion, going shopping together, then holding impromptu cooking lessons.

Soon the parents of new babies had meals provided for two weeks. Permission was obtained to set up buffets in people's homes after funeral services. New people came to faith in Christ, attracted by how well the body of believers cared for each other in times of need. As the church grew, the meals ministry eventually involved more than two hundred people and ran on essentially no budget. Through identifying and providing missing resources such as an administrator, volunteers, cooking skills, and money, Effie built a successful, growing, and life-transforming ministry.

ROBERT E. LOGAN | LOGANLEADERSHIP.COM

Along the way we celebrated successes, addressed challenges, and figured out next steps. Together, those two women built a care team that mobilized hundreds of people to bring meals after funerals or at the births of babies or to visit the sick in hospitals. God did incredible things through their ministry.

> **There are few investments you can make that will produce more fruit for the kingdom of God than truly developing and empowering new leaders.**

By providing targeted support for key leaders, you can build ministries much more diverse and powerful than what you could do on your own. There are few investments you can make that will produce more fruit for the kingdom of God than truly developing and empowering new leaders. To do that, you'll need to provide intensive supervision, coaching, and development to the people on your team.

We see this same kind of intentional development of new leaders in scripture. Priscilla and Aquila had worked and traveled extensively with the apostle Paul, and we see how they then began investing in and sponsoring Apollos:

> *Meanwhile a Jew named Apollos, a native of Alexandria, came to Ephesus. He was a learned man, with a thorough knowledge of the Scriptures. He had been instructed in the way of the Lord, and he spoke with great fervor and taught about Jesus accurately, though he knew only the baptism of John. He began to speak boldly in the synagogue. When Priscilla and Aquila heard him, they invited him to their home and explained to him the way of God more adequately.*

> *When Apollos wanted to go to Achaia, the brothers and sisters encouraged him and wrote to the disciples there to welcome him. When he arrived, he was a great help to those who by grace had believed. For he vigorously refuted his Jewish opponents in public debate, proving from the Scriptures that Jesus was the Messiah (Acts 18:24–28).*

Due in part to their investment in and support of Apollos, we see how effective he became in ministry. If you really want to develop the people on your team, you need provide a clear, intentional process that includes supervision, coaching, feedback, skill development practice, and a clear development plan. It's an investment.

Topics we'll cover include:

- Intentionality
- Skill development
- The orient-involve-equip process
- The supervision coaching cycle
- Providing feedback
- Facilitating communication within your team

Intentionality

The entire process of intensive people development is built on a foundation of intentionality. Most people have good intentions; we want to do a better job of coming alongside our leaders and equipping them for ministry. But good intentions aren't enough. They need to be translated into action. We need to put a process in place and get traction moving forward—and that's not always easy to do.

> Good intentions aren't enough. They need to be translated into action.

The shift that needs to happen is to move from good intentions to becoming intentional.

One pastor I know asks each of his staff members to respond to these five questions each week:

1. What did I hear God say to me this week?

2. What is the most important thing I need to accomplish this week?

3. Who is the one person I need to invest in this week?

4. What is the one thing our community needs from us as leaders this week?

5. Is there one "sbag" (stretching but achievable goal) that we should pursue this week?

These questions help them crystallize what they feel God calling them to do in the next week. The key question for the senior leader to reflect on is this: "How can you intentionalize what you're doing, to create environments and processes that allow optimal people development to happen?"

A note from Colin:

An issue of Business Week noted that, in his seventeen years as the CEO of General Electric, Jack Welch developed fifteen thousand new executive leaders. Peter Drucker reminds us that "there may be born leaders—but there are far too few of them to depend on."

The future of any organisation depends on intentional leadership development. This is not only a need, but it is also biblical. Developing leaders formed the crux of Jesus' ministry as he prepared the disciples for the biggest task in history. God is in the business of developing leaders, and he continues the process throughout their entire lifetimes. People are an organisation's most important resource, yet most churches and parachurches use people; they do not develop them.

Skill development

One area to be particularly intentional about is the development of skills. As a developer of others, you want to provide opportunity for your leaders to learn and practice new skills. That involves a certain risk on your part, as new leaders will not be fully competent and will sometimes fail. They may not be able to do everything the way you would do it, but that's part of the price of development.

You can minimize the risk to some degree, such as by letting a developing public speaker practice in a smaller, less formal environment rather than by beginning with a sermon. But you can't mitigate the risk all together. Skill development takes time and practice—and affirmation.

For me, seminary preaching classes were a painful experience. The worst part was when I had to go to the preaching lab to be videotaped as I struggled to deliver a message. Having to listen to myself on tape seemed bad enough, but having to see myself too was just too much.

My school had some video technicians who were rumored to find a prospective preacher's bad habits or mannerisms—and zoom the cameras in on them. For instance, if your hands imitated "spiders doing pushups on a mirror," it was circulating among students that the videographers would actually fill the screen with your hands. If these guys ever decided to produce a film called *What Not to Do When Preaching*, you can just imagine all the raw footage we gave them to work with.

As I had tried to learn how to become more comfortable preaching in front of an audience, I seemed to get worse rather than better. I had to give multiple sermons, receiving feedback on them from the professor and the other students. As I became aware of my blunders, I put more and more pressure on myself. The more I practiced my preaching, the worse I got. I was in a downward spiral when the time came for me to be videotaped.

When my video was ready for viewing, I dragged myself into the lab and there was a new technician there. As we watched the videotapes together, Randy would make a comment from time to time: "Nice use of words there." "Good transition." He commented on the positives. Sometimes he had long pauses between those comments, but he only said good things.

At the end of the segment, Randy shut off the recorder and said, "Bob, let me share with you your three greatest strengths in speaking," and he went on to list them. When he finished, Randy made one more comment that transformed my communication ability and my confidence: "You don't get better by focusing on your weaknesses. You get better by accentuating your strengths." If I focused on my strong points, explained Randy, the weaknesses would tend to disappear over time. This revolutionary perspective freed me to concentrate on what I did well, and my preaching skills improved dramatically.

Don't underestimate the value of helping people improve by focusing on what they do well. Point people toward basic competence, certainly, but remember that positive reinforcement can work wonders as you develop your people.

From there, people will grow in confidence through practice. Start slowly and begin from wherever they are. To continue the previous example of public speaking, you could ask a new leader to give a short talk, such as a devotional or a testimony. Most leaders will be expected to be able to do this regardless of gifting, so help them be prepared to put together and deliver a brief talk.

They should be able to read a Scripture passage aloud, make a few observations about it, then wrap it up with a conclusion or restatement of the main point.

Smaller talks such as this are often a first step with getting more comfortable with larger public speaking projects. As people speak more often, they will become more comfortable talking in front of groups and they will improve. Encourage continued practice.

Applied to any type of ministry skill, the cycle looks like this:

- You do the ministry.
- You model the ministry for others.
- You do ministry alongside others and provide feedback.
- Others do the ministry on their own and you get together to discuss it.

This time spent in reflection is essential, as it allows for the input of others and time for listening to the Holy Spirit. This method of gradual release creates an effective way to train others to do the work of the ministry. We need to do training in the context of relationship—life-on-life, with room for conversation and questions.

The orient-involve-equip process

Here's another framework you can use for developing people. I call it orient, involve, equip.

Orienting is not full-blown training. It is simply establishing the framework for what's expected. It is sharing the vision for a ministry and establishing a common understanding of what is supposed to be done and why. Orienting can involve a classroom component, but is better done through modeling, observation, and intentional debriefing conversations.

For example, if you are training a leader in how to facilitate a small group, you could invite her to observe you facilitating a group and then have a conversation afterward, where you could unpack her observations and answer her questions. People absorb at least twice as much this way as they do in classroom training—plus they have a concrete picture of what the ministry looks like. They may make adaptations, but they can model their own group after yours.

Involving means moving the person you're developing from an observing posture to a helping posture. You're still there, you're still leading, but they're now helping. They can do ministry alongside you, with close supervision and guidance.

In a small-group facilitator training process, you could give the volunteer various tasks of increasing difficulty. One week he could lead the prayer time. Another week he could lead the Scripture discussion. Maybe he could plan a group service project. Eventually, he would be doing all of the pieces of facilitating a small group.

Equipping is the debriefing stage, where the leader you're training can ask questions, share insights, and reflect on learnings. These are the over-coffee conversations after the group has ended. Because the leader has been knee-deep in ministry already, she knows the questions to ask and is primed to pay close attention to the answers: "What should I do when that guy is monopolizing the conversation?" "How can I gain more buy-in for the group service project?"

As the leader becomes more and more proficient in facilitating the group, the equipping stage moves seamlessly into a coaching relationship. You no longer need to be attending the group with him. Instead, you're coaching him in his own ministry. Both ownership and leadership have been passed on.

A note from Colin:

As people grow in leadership confidence, they should be allowed and encouraged to move into more complex ministries. The skills required by an apprentice small-group leader are different from those needed by someone who oversees twenty small groups.

Current leaders often get lost in this transition because their own understanding is pushed to the limit. When this happens, I have observed two things. First, the leader subconsciously holds the potential leader to his own level of competency. Second, he tries to help but recommends that these potential leaders read three-hundred-page books. If a potential leader grows beyond where you are, rejoice with him. Help him find succinct resource materials. Put him in touch with others who are able to continue their growth. The kingdom will be the beneficiary.

The supervision/coaching cycle

However, when you pass on ministry to others, that doesn't mean you step out of the mix entirely. You still need to provide support, and a big part of providing ongoing support is simply being around. Are you available? Are you reachable if a new leader needs you? Does she know she can reach out if there's an issue? New leaders shouldn't feel micromanaged, but they shouldn't feel abandoned either. Make the open-door policy clear—and budget some time for it.

Yet be aware that most leaders won't seek you out unless something goes very wrong—and by then it's often too late. You'll also need to intentionally set aside time to check in with new leaders to see how it's going. Especially if you are leading a staff team, there are two distinct ways of doing this: supervision and coaching.

A supervisor needs to hold the person accountable for results, work toward agreement on goals, and evaluate progress. A coach, on the other hand, needs to draw out and help support the person's own ideas. You can see the potential conflict, I'm sure. The more you wear the supervisor hat, the more you create the temptation to micromanage. Yet the supervisor role is needed— for selecting leaders, for defining their job roles, for deciding what results need to be accomplished, for determining how and when progress will be evaluated, for developing growth plans, and for holding people accountable for the results they're supposed to be getting.

Part of the challenge within many churches that implement coaching for their staff is that they often don't have the luxury of separating the coaching and the supervision functions. In many churches, the supervisor is the one who is providing the coaching. That can be challenging, as it's difficult for many staff people to confide their difficulties and challenges to the same person who is evaluating their job performance.

Although this issue will always create tension to some degree, it can be helped by creating a rhythm that separates the two roles. The first step is to separate the sessions. If you try to provide both coaching and supervision within the same session, it gets muddled and you often don't get accomplished what you want to accomplish. A key to making this division work is clearly laying out which conversations are which.

Let's say you meet with each leader on an individual basis monthly. For staff-level people, you probably only need to have three supervisory meetings per year. Every four months, they can come prepared to share what's been accomplished in the last four months. They can also provide their priorities and specific goals for the next four months. The supervisor, of course, has the chance to speak into that, and also give a performance review. Between your every-four-month supervision appointments is where you want your three coaching conversions.

Those coaching conversations come with the agenda, because the staff member already knows what he is trying to accomplish. The task at hand now is processing and determining what kind of help or support is needed. In this way, you're working seventy-five percent of your time in a developmental mode, and twenty-five percent of your time in supervision mode. What I'm suggesting— and what has worked well—is to create this type of rhythm: Schedule three supervisory appointments per year: January, May, and September. Functionally, you're on a trimester system. In between supervision appointments, schedule those nine monthly coaching appointments.

Annual supervision and coaching cycle

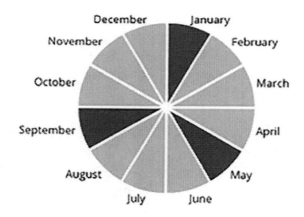

During the coaching appointments, be sure you're clearly wearing the coaching hat and that the agenda is totally their prerogative. They already know what they're supposed to be accomplishing; they have clarity on what they're responsible for. During these sessions, they determine what is most helpful to process with you. Instead of giving advice or directives, ask, "So what have you already thought of?" Unpack their answers fully before giving any input. You don't need to do their thinking for them. They are not looking to you for answers. They are responsible for their own thinking and actions to do what needs to be done. By your holding a very clear coaching posture, you can help them use these times more effectively.

Supervision tasks	Coaching tasks
Communicate clearly when supervision will take place	Listen
	Reflect back what you are hearing
Clarify expected outcomes and goals in advance	Ask good questions
Separate *what* the leader is trying to accomplish from *how* they're trying to accomplish it	Facilitate brainstorming
	Help the leader determine a course of action
Evaluate progress	Provide resources as needed
Affirm and stretch	Encourage and pray

Providing feedback

We all need others who can speak into our lives, tell us the potential they see, and help us examine our blind spots. We need people we can bounce our ideas off and get their first impressions. We need people who can reflect back to us what they are seeing. As someone who is involved in intensive development of leaders, being that person for others is part of your role. People need formative feedback in order to keep growing.

 Formative feedback is helping people see what they can do better next time: a new skill they might try incorporating, a good direction for the future. Always start with specific affirmations; and when providing corrective feedback, try to link it to something they're doing well so they can build off their strengths.

Sometimes when people hear "feedback," their minds go quickly to "criticism." But true and helpful feedback means reflecting back both the positive and negative things you see. Actually, positive reinforcement should far outweigh any type of negative feedback. For the goal is growth and wisdom:

> My son, if you accept my words
> and store up my commands within you,
> turning your ear to wisdom
> and applying your heart to understanding—
> indeed, if you call out for insight
> and cry aloud for understanding,
> and if you look for it as for silver
> and search for it as for hidden treasure,
> then you will understand the fear of the Lord
> and find the knowledge of God.
> For the Lord gives wisdom;
> from his mouth come knowledge and understanding (Prov. 2:1–6).

A note from Colin:

Although the idea is not his invention, coach and author Marshall Goldsmith has popularised an approach that can be used beside traditional feedback. He calls this process "feed-forward." He contends that feedback requires a historical perspective and thereby concentrates on what can only be learned from but not changed. By looking forward positively, we set ourselves free from what's happened before—we allow a fresh start. The rules of the "feed-forward" process are very simple:

- *Ask the growing leader to identify one or two key changes or actions he or she wants to make.*

- *Make all your questions about future possible changes. Focus on the future, not the past, e.g., say "Could you. . . ?"*

- *Listen to ideas without clarification, and just respond by saying "thank you" before asking for another idea.*

Offering feedback is an important part of how any coach communicates with a leader. However, by adding the "feed-forward" approach, we can often more readily help an individual to open up new possibilities for the future.

Pastors and other Christian leaders are often in a position to hear positive statements about people who serve alongside them: "The music has been amazing lately... so much energy!" or "My son has been loving his Sunday school class; he talks about it all week at home." Make sure you pass on every compliment you can to your staff members or others on your team. The reinforcement of their actions will encourage them to continue those actions, and hearing when others appreciate your work is motivating to everyone.

When I was a senior pastor, I would give informal feedback on a consistent basis to each staff person I oversaw, but once a year I would sit down for a formal annual review with each member of my staff. I began by giving them an evaluation form that they were to fill out before our meeting. It covered these categories:

- List your areas of responsibility, along with a rating of each one on a scale of 1–10

- List your strengths

- A rating on a scale of 1–10 for their personal job satisfaction

- A rating on a scale of 1–10 for their overall effectiveness

- List your growth areas

- Write your action plan in a few lines

- Any additional comments

They filled out the form about themselves and I filled out the form about them (except for their personal job satisfaction). Then at the in-person meeting, we would fill out a new form together. Sometimes the differences in perspective were eye-opening.

I was intentional about not listing their areas of responsibility on the form for them. They just saw seven blanks and were to fill in what they saw as their responsibilities. I wanted *them* to articulate what they were doing and how effective they felt they were in each of those areas.

Sometimes I would find out they were doing some things I wasn't aware they were doing—really good things. In other cases, I found out things they were doing that didn't really need to be done. These discoveries led to some helpful conversations about what they were doing and why. When we had agreed on a list of responsibilities, we went through each one and talked about specific examples of what it currently looked like.

When we talked about their strengths, I was always sure to add two or three that they hadn't identified.

Under personal job satisfaction, no matter what they wrote, I'd ask, "How could it be higher?" Often, there were some simple solutions. Maybe someone needed to get information from me in a timelier matter, so that he could do his job more effectively. Maybe someone needed to start and end their day a bit earlier on Wednesdays to make it to her kid's soccer game. Sometimes I would discover stress or conflict between him and another person, and I would help him walk through that.

The staff review time was never scary or threatening for people, because it was development-based, not performance-based. The purpose was largely for affirmation and growth. Where did they want to grow? What new skills did they want to develop? I found that with this approach, no one feared the job reviews. It was an affirming environment focused on developing them to their fullest potential. In some cases, these reviews even moved people into new areas of responsibility that were more in line with how God had wired them.

We'd end by creating a personal development plan based on their goals. This means deciding on specific, measurable goals together, and then following up on progress toward those the next time we'd meet.

Facilitating communication within your team

Ensuring your team is communicating well with you and each other can be a moving target; it's something you need to keep revisiting periodically.

Good communication includes making sure each member of your team is continuing to improve their basic communication skills—things like listening well, asking good questions, giving feedback appropriately, and speaking directly to the people involved when there is conflict. There are also times when you may need to mediate conflict among your team members when their own efforts have not succeeded. You can review some of these skills in the chapter on communication and train your team on them.

Another important element of strong communication within a team is being sure everyone is clear on each member's strengths, roles, responsibilities, and contributions. A working understanding of this information helps everyone be clear on the connections between different roles and the places where those roles overlap.

For instance, in many church structures there is a clear connection between the leader who oversees the greeting team and the leader who oversees the small groups. The idea is to help newcomers get connected and become part of a small group where they will be known and cared for. These two leaders must communicate well and be clear about how and when people will be handed off from one ministry to the next—when someone ceases to be a newcomer and becomes an integrated part of a small group.

One of the most helpful things I've found for building solid teams is to make a clear distinction between responsibility and contribution. Responsibility is the job—what people are responsible for. If it doesn't get accomplished, they are held responsible because it was a clear part of their responsibility. However, I found that within a team, too much focus on one's own area of responsibility creates a silo effect. Each person works only in his or her own area of responsibility and doesn't see how it connects with other areas or other team members.

> **A note from Colin:**
>
> One of the most effective ways I have found to facilitate communication within a team, especially as the church gets bigger, is to create what Carl George calls a Leadership Axis Team. The team meets regularly (weekly in larger teams), and each leader reports on his or her sphere of ministry (responsibility) especially when it comes to people, resources, and time. This is followed by an open discussion on how decisions (especially related to change) in this ministry will affect the other spheres of ministry in the church. This may include some compromise but—if it is done around values, mission, and vision—the team moves forward as one and avoids silo behaviour.

One way to facilitate this kind of connection among team members is to spend focused time on each person to identify their core strength, their area of responsibility, and the main contribution they could bring to the broader ministry. Taking the time to pinpoint this also allows time for them to be affirmed. For instance, somebody might have a real strength in sensitivity to newcomers—events or environments that are welcoming to newcomers. Another team member might have a strength in helping organize something into a system. The whole team can pinpoint and affirm these areas, which then forms the basis for that person's contribution.

Here's the process I use:

1. Go through each person to determine their strengths, their responsibilities within their role, and their potential contribution to the broader ministry.

2. Affirm those areas together with the whole team.

3. Give permission for each person to point out something in their area of strength, or contribution to another leader—as long as they also offer to assist that other leader and come alongside them as a consultant to help.

4. Give everyone permission to ask others for help in their respective areas of strength or contribution.

Name of team member	Strengths	Responsibilities	Contributions

Let's say a staff member has strengths in hospitality and as a connector of people. Her area of responsibility is to oversee the newcomer's class. Yet her area of contribution could be to help other ministry areas create welcoming environments for newcomers. She could say something like, "I see some ways we could make your ministry area a bit more welcoming for newcomers. Would you be willing to have me come alongside and help you with that?" In that way, the offer is not just one of critique but one of help as well. She's contributing to the team by offering her help and her strengths.

Note that this approach only works when the team, as a whole, has already clarified each person's areas of strength, responsibility, and contribution. In that case, it utilizes people across the broader ministry system to contribute beyond just their area of responsibility, creating a much stronger team overall.

> When a team is working together well, it can help each member begin to see through each other's eyes.

When a team is working together well, it can help each member begin to see through each other's eyes. We can more easily put ourselves in someone else's shoes and understand what matters to them and how they think. This effort not only helps us love others well, but it helps us not become calcified into our own views and perspectives—becoming inflexible like the Pharisees. It's good for us to stretch our minds and try to see through other people's eyes—and often we can learn a great deal.

Developing others to their fullest capacity means that at some point God may call them elsewhere. As senior leaders, we need to develop people with a kingdom mindset foremost in our thoughts. We are not raising up more leaders to help our own ministry—although they may; we are raising them up to help God's ministry in the world, which is so much broader than our own little corner of it. We need to hold our people with open hands, knowing that God may call them onward without us. That may hurt, both professionally and personally, but we can also look at it as an extension of our own investments and efforts going forth into the world.

Prayer guide

- Who is God calling you to invest in? What challenges and risks does that present for you?

- Take some time for reflection on the current strengths of each of your team members. What do you see?

- How can you be more intentional about developing the leaders you oversee?

- What approach to coaching and supervision might work best in your context?

- How willing are you to develop someone, and then release him or her to another ministry?

For further reading:

- *The Trusted Advisor*, by David H. Maister and Charles H. Green

- *The First 90 Days: Proven Strategies for Getting Up to Speed Faster and Smarter,* by Michael D. Watkins

- *Influencer: The New Science of Leading Change*, by Grenny/ Patterson/Maxfield/ McMillan/Switzler

ORGANIZATIONAL DEVELOPMENT

Shifting Gears to Avoid Stalling Out

A year or two into our plant, as the church grew, I knew we'd have to start doing some things differently to help us organize. I brought in an outside consultant to help us understand and prepare for these changes. One of the first things he did was ask me to complete a behavioral-style assessment: the DiSC. This assessment is designed to identify people's work styles in the context of their teams. Better understanding your work style—and those of others—helps you build more effective working relationships. The DiSC letters stand for Dominance, Influence, Steadiness and Conscientiousness. (You can find out more about the DiSC profile online.)

For anyone who knows the assessment and knows me, it will come as no surprise that I scored as a high D: the dominant, results-oriented type. A few things about Ds: We are driven high-pressure people who value results, we want to get things accomplished, and if you turn us loose we'll get things done and plow through obstacles. Sounded good to me.

Yet the consultant's first words to me on receiving these assessment results were: "Bob, if you don't adapt your behavior, you will kill this church."

His words were direct, blunt, and tapped into the core motivation I had for results. I wanted to grow the church. I wanted to reach people for Jesus. Because I valued those results, he had my attention. (You must always get a D's attention before giving them feedback.) That's why I was willing to ask him the obvious follow-up question: "What do you mean?"

> "Bob, if you don't adapt your behavior, you will kill this church."

Apparently, along with the pluses of being a D come certain minuses as well. For instance, Ds are notorious for selective listening: listening only insofar as it directly bears on our goals. We can be driven, not giving people breaks or building in time for rest, and skipping the celebration of accomplishments in favor of moving on toward the next goal. We can be direct to the point of bluntness.

As the consultant explained it, I needed to understand who I was working with and flex my behavior accordingly, in order to get better results. My task orientation was driving people into the ground. I needed to learn how to adapt my style to work effectively with people who were different than me. I began to learn to listen to people better, ask questions, and build relationships.

Over the next eighteen to twenty-four months, I very painfully, step by step, learned how to flex my behavior to get results in a way that was appropriate for others as well. When I held team meetings, I would actually write down on my agenda, "Be relational." I even put down a timeframe: twenty minutes. I didn't show anyone else this agenda, of course. I'd also add notes: "Ask so-and-so about his brother," or some other relational item unconnected to the task at hand. On my calendar, I'd write at random intervals, "Call so-and-so and encourage her."

Sound artificial? Absolutely. I was forcing myself to learn a new set of behaviors that did not come at all naturally to me. Yet over time, these behaviors became habits and I could do them without as much effort. But remember—it did take eighteen to twenty-four months.

> **A note from Colin:**
>
> *Bob's journey started by recognizing who he was. Remember, "different" doesn't equal wrong; "different" equals different. Bob discovered he was results-oriented. Others will discover they strive for personal recognition, appreciation, or correctness.*
>
> *It is also important to remember that what Bob is explaining here is flexing—not necessarily behavioural change. Too much flexing over an extended period of time will cause problems, including stress or subconscious denial. I have known Bob for a long time; there is no doubt that he has been able to flex some of his behavior, but let me assure you that he is still a "D."*

Your own needed adjustments may look considerably different than mine. But the point is, you will need to make some. Consider what the other person needs, and how you can flex your behavior to help meet that need.

This chapter is all about how you will need to change your approach as the organization grows, in order to be positioned for maximum effectiveness. Although changes to individual leadership styles may vary, one constant is that you'll need to involve more people in leadership. We see this reality throughout Scripture as well:

> *And the things you have heard me say in the presence of many witnesses entrust to reliable people who will also be qualified to teach others (2 Tim. 2:2).*

In those days when the number of disciples was increasing, the Hellenistic Jews among them complained against the Hebraic Jews because their widows were being overlooked in the daily distribution of food. So the Twelve gathered all the disciples together and said, "It would not be right for us to neglect the ministry of the word of God in order to wait on tables. Brothers and sisters, choose seven men from among you who are known to be full of the Spirit and wisdom. We will turn this responsibility over to them and will give our attention to prayer and the ministry of the word."

This proposal pleased the whole group. They chose Stephen, a man full of faith and of the Holy Spirit; also Philip, Procorus, Nicanor, Timon, Parmenas, and Nicolas from Antioch, a convert to Judaism. They presented these men to the apostles, who prayed and laid their hands on them.

So the word of God spread. The number of disciples in Jerusalem increased rapidly, and a large number of priests became obedient to the faith (Acts 6:1–7).

As Peter Drucker says, "The most common cause of executive failure is inability or unwillingness to change with the demands of a new position." When you're in a new position—or when the growth of the organization demands a different approach—the contribution that brought you success previously is probably not the same one that will bring you success now. As your ministry organization grows and develops, you need to shift gears in order to avoid stalling out. Staying in the same gear—when a different one is required—will lead to ineffectiveness. Gear-shifting is essential for going on to the next phase.

> **As your ministry organization grows and develops, you need to shift gears in order to avoid stalling out.**

Topics covered in this chapter include:
- Broadening the span of care
- Facilitating shepherding
- Overseeing small groups
- Modifying the plan as you go
- Getting a coach
- Identifying a successor

Broadening the span of care

As your organization grows, you'll see a bigger need for structure. What just seemed to work organically before no longer works without some planning. As the senior leader, you'll increasingly need to work *on* the ministry rather than *in* it. In most cases that means getting some perspective and distance from the direct work itself.

However, one of the most common problems in a church environment is the widespread perception that the pastor is directly in charge of everything. I ran into this barrier as a senior pastor, and had to be quite intentional about ridding myself of those expectations. When I realized I was doing too much myself, I put a new structure in place with other overseers in charge of various ministry areas. The idea was to reorganize and reduce the span of care. But I found that people were still calling me whenever they wanted to know something. My phone was ringing all the time. (Today the issue would probably be an overflowing email inbox, but this was pre-Internet.)

Obviously, something additional needed to be done. I decided to stop answering any questions that were not my direct responsibility. When people called to ask what time the prayer meeting was, I'd say, "So-and-so is now in charge of that. They can get you the information you need." After about six months, the phone stopped ringing and word got around the church that Logan didn't know anything.

This rumor was verified one Easter Sunday when a new person came up to me in the lobby. She asked me where the Easter egg hunt was. I honestly didn't know we were having an Easter egg hunt, so I told her I didn't know. She laughed and said, "I asked Kim where it was and she didn't know. So I told her 'I'll just ask the pastor.' She said, 'Oh no, don't do that. Bob doesn't know anything.'" Apparently, Kim was right.

By limiting what I was directly responsible for, I was able to focus on what I was supposed to be doing, and on the new leaders I needed to be investing in. Too often senior leaders short-circuit the process by taking on more responsibility than we need to. We keep burdening ourselves, and at the same time disempowering our people. The key is increasing the span of care and releasing more responsibility and authority to others.

Facilitating shepherding

An important piece of expanding the span of care is to spread shepherding responsibilities among a broader group of people. As leaders of the church, we are responsible for shepherding the people: "Keep watch over yourselves and all the flock of which the

> Overseeing something to make sure it is happening is not the same thing as doing it all yourself.

Holy Spirit has made you overseers. Be shepherds of the church of God, which he bought with his own blood" (Acts 20:28).

A church or ministry is not the same as a secular organization. It's not only about the vision. A church or ministry also takes care of its people. For centuries, pastors have shepherded their people from the cradle to the grave and all the steps in between. And that truly matters. Yet overseeing something to make sure it is happening is not the same thing as doing it all yourself. Just as it is in literal shepherding, a lot depends on the size of the flock.

When I say shepherding, I mean general pastoral care (which doesn't need to be given directly by a pastor, but the pastor is responsible to make sure it *is* being provided). It includes things like helping the hurting, listening, and encouraging. It can often look like praying with people or visiting them in the hospital. It also includes some gentle directing... letting the sheep know where to go and where not to go... providing correction for the sake of the sheep's safety. When people are going down a bad path, we are to warn them. We can come alongside them and gently redirect them back onto a good path for their own good and flourishing.

A note from Colin:

The shift required by church leaders as growth occurs is very difficult. Research shows that ninety to ninety-five percent of ministers begin their ministry as pastors. Following are some of the most common characteristics of pastors. Remember, what they do is not wrong; it is the focus of their behaviour, not their hearts.

- *Primary care giving. Pastors try to be the major care providers for the entire church. When they come across a need they ask, "How will I meet it?"*

- *Live in the moment. Their preoccupation with crisis intervention, hospital calls, and other pastoral acts prevents them seeing that support roles are essential for effective ministry.*

- *Driven by expectation. Pastors attempt to meet all expectations by being omnipresent. They feel bound to attend every meeting or program, lest they hear the disappointing news, "It just wasn't the same without you" (meaning, "you have created a dependency syndrome"). As a result, others set the agenda for their ministry and life.*

- *Availability. They think in terms of how they can be more accessible. They convey to the church that they will be available for whatever is necessary. Many problems in the pastor's family stem from this attitude.*

Shepherding well also includes teaching others how to shepherd. One of the ways to provide care is to raise up more shepherds. Because this role is by nature time-consuming, you cannot expect only a handful of leaders to provide shepherding for a congregation. Mobilize others to help, and consider how you could teach them shepherding skills.

I was never a natural at some of the "standard" pastoral skills. I wasn't sure what to say on hospital visits or what to do at weddings. For many pastors, those skills come easily, but not for me. Fortunately, the church I attended in my early twenties placed me in an internship position, where they had a system in place for teaching pastoral care skills. My job was to follow around some of the pastors as they did hospital visits, weddings, funerals, and counseling people after the services. I went with them and watched what they did. Then I got a chance to take the lead and try out some of those new skills, with the pastors watching. Afterward we would talk about some of the ways I could do it more effectively. The next time I did it, I tried to do what they had suggested, and slowly I could see my competence level rising.

It's always worth developing and investing in your people—even if we don't all seem like naturals at first. Some related skills in this book you may want to cross reference here are the sections on delegating and on developing leaders.

Overseeing small groups

In its earliest form, the church met in small groups. It still meets that way throughout the world today in many places. Small groups allow people to know each other and be known, pray together, learn together, and encourage and challenge one another on toward love and good deeds. These smaller communities form the core of Christian community.

A note from Colin:

If you have no small groups in your church (or your church is less than seventy people) and you want to grow this ministry, here are some suggested steps:

- ***Up to 70 people***: *Form a small group and personally lead it—raise up a new leader and multiply your small group.*

- ***Between 70 and 120 people***: *Continue to personally lead a small group—nurture, train, and resource a number of small group leaders—start more small groups.*

- ***Between 120 and 200 people***: *Continue to personally lead a small group—continue to nurture, train, and resource small group leaders—multiply small groups continually.*

Leading these groups well as the organization grows is critical. Early on in a church's growth—as soon as a church has enough people for more than two or three small groups—the pastor cannot lead all of the groups personally. The same is true in other types of ministries. You will need to develop others who can lead them and provide support for the people. What are the key components to train others in for this important role?

First, recognize that it's not just about teaching. People learn best through dialogue, action, and considering questions. Gear your small groups around these principles. Encourage your group facilitators to ask people questions, let them ponder, let them make guesses and consider ideas—even if it's outside the bounds of your particular theology. That's how people learn.

> It's this life-on-life living out of the Christian faith that helps people experience God in tangible ways.

Never say something you can get others to come up with. That's the role of a facilitator.

A facilitator should also foster action. Is someone in the group sick or in crisis? How can others in the group serve them? How can the group serve the surrounding community? What can the group pray for or do together? It's this life-on-life living out of the Christian faith that helps people experience God in tangible ways.

Additionally, small group leaders will need to:

- **Ask good questions.** Never make a statement when you can ask a question instead. The point of a small group format is to be able to draw others out so they can talk. It's not teaching time. It's not a sermon. It's a discussion, and questions help facilitate that discussion.

- **Model vulnerability**. If you're leading a group, people will look to you to see what they should be doing. How much should they share and at what level? If you take the lead in sharing some challenges you face, others will feel comfortable doing the same. If you pretend to have it all together, others will follow suit.

- **Help people feel heard.** Provide enough space in the group for everyone to get enough air time. This ensures that people have time to talk, process their ideas, and feel heard. Even if you have no solutions for people's problems, it's amazing what the power of feeling heard can do.

- **Build community.** Find ways to support one another. Encourage one another in times and difficulty, celebrate important milestones, provide offers of practical support when it's needed. A small group is about much more than any content you're studying. It's about the relationships and the community that are being formed and the extent to which they reflect Jesus.

- **Gain ownership.** Just because you're leading or facilitating a group doesn't mean you should be doing everything. There are plenty of ways others can share in the ownership of the group. They could bring snacks, plan social events, lead the prayer time, prepare service projects the group can participate in together. The more others are helping with the leadership of the group, the more ownership you have. It's not *your* group, but *our* group.

Most importantly, as you empower others to lead small groups and provide care for people through those groups, it will mean letting go of the role yourself. You won't be directly able to pastor all of the people as the ministry grows. However, you can still make sure everyone—including those leading the groups—are being pastored and cared for. We can look to the way Jesus invested in the twelve disciples and the way he served the crowds as our model.

Modifying the plan as you go

As your ministry grows, you'll be engaged in a constant cycle of planning, seeing where the growth takes you, and then adjusting that plan. Don't worry about making sure all the details are completely clear before you set out. It's almost a certainty that the plan will need to be changed as you go.

As leaders, we can watch for this dynamic by monitoring and evaluating progress. If some areas are going well, how can we make best use of that momentum? What principles can we apply to other areas? What more can we invest in what is working? Likewise, if some areas are not progressing as we had hoped, what can we do to improve matters? How can we determine the core problem? How might we redirect our energy instead?

A note from Colin:

To ensure good monitoring and evaluating, we need to be clear on the measurements we are using and that we are measuring the right things. The leadership writer Warren Bennis once described the difference between management and leadership as follows:

"Management is climbing the rungs of the ladder as fast as we can. Leadership is making sure that the ladder is leaning against the right wall."

If you apply the same principle to your plans and their measurement, it is more important to make sure that you are measuring the right things, than it is to gather evidence of fantastic progress in an area that has little bearing on the achievement of your overall vision. Here is an example: If you plan to double the amount of time you spend with your children within the next twelve months, and then achieve that by sitting in the same room watching television, you have probably missed the point. The measure of quantity (exact count of hours spent in their vicinity) may indicate you were successful, but you also need to use the measure of quality, e.g., by considering "how many more conversations I had with my son about topics that are important to him."

We'll need to adapt to continually changing circumstances and environments. The world in which we are carrying out our plans is not static. What seems like a good strategy one day may be a terrible strategy the next if the situation has changed. For example, say you have a celebration planned, but a national tragedy takes place the day before. You may need to modify. That could mean canceling the event, rescheduling it, or changing the way you present it. Context and conditions matter, and sometimes we must shift course in response.

Even unexpected successes can cause modifications in plans. Let's say a church was planning to focus on financial stewardship for this next ministry season. That's certainly a fine plan. But then let's say a recent influx of refugees was being resettled near where the church meets. There's a lot of energy around the issue and people desiring

> **Context and conditions matter, and sometimes we must shift course in response.**

to get involved and help. In that case, it may make sense to capitalize on that energy and focus on serving the refugee community in practical ways. And as an aside: What a great perspective the congregation will be getting on stewardship!

Many mistakes have been made by creating and implementing a plan—and then sticking to it even when it's become clear that the plan isn't working as intended. Rather, we need to periodically assess and reevaluate to see where to invest our energy as we see what God is doing. As you review progress, celebrate wins and confirm what's working. Identify obstacles and decide where to focus your energy next.

This strategy is a real-world approach to changing ministry situations. In the book of Nehemiah, we see a plan unfolding and changing to adapt to the context as it arises. Nehemiah gets a vision from God to repair the walls of Jerusalem, gets permissions and blessings from the king he serves, travels to Jerusalem and inspires the people to begin rebuilding. He organizes and divides the work, and begins implementing it. When he becomes aware of a plot to thwart the rebuilding of the walls, he adapts his plan to include defense. Nehemiah also handled internal problems and complaints from the people. He helped establish and reform the governance of the people and foiled plots from the enemies. Read through the book of Nehemiah sometime, to observe the dexterity and leadership skills with which he led a growing movement. There's a lot we can learn.

Some related skills in this book you may want to cross-reference here are the sections on goal-setting (chapter 7), planning (chapter 7), and leading change (chapter 8).

Getting a coach

If you are leading a growing organization that you want to steer toward health and the accomplishment of mission, you absolutely need a coach. Virtually all leaders have good intentions. You want to see good things happen. You want to see people get into discipleship relationships. You want to see people experience authentic life change. You want to do a better job of coming alongside your leaders and equipping them for ministry. Nobody wants to be ineffective; nobody wants to fail.

But good intentions aren't enough. If you want to translate them into action and maximize results, you need a coach. All leaders need to get traction and move forward—and that's not easy to do alone. *The shift that needs to happen is moving from good intentions to becoming intentional.* That means getting a coach who can help you create a plan, take wise steps, get traction, and see results. Many leaders just hope for good things to happen, but they're not actualizing those good intentions in a way that actually gets them there.

Coaching is a way to help you intentionalize your actions, in a way that gets you where you want to go. A coach wants to see you focus your energy in a clear direction. Consider: What have you hoped would be happening in your life and ministry for months and years now that just hasn't really happened? How serious are you about it? What steps could you take if you were really serious? Maybe it's time to consider a coaching relationship.

> **Coaching is a way to help you intentionalize your actions, in a way that gets you where you want to go.**

Most leaders want their ministries to grow. But that means dealing with change—and that's hard. Prices will need to be paid. So often people want change, but they want it to be easy. A coach can help you determine if you *really* want the change—and if you want it badly enough to be willing to pay the price.

A coach is not a mentor or a guru. They don't need to know everything and they don't need to have direct experience with the situation you're dealing with. However, they should be able to ask you good questions, to make you think through how to shift gears as your organization grows. They should provide perspective and help you look at factors you may not have considered.

Identifying a successor

In addition to having a coach to help guide you as your organization grows, you'll want to look the other direction too: toward a successor. Even if you have no current plans to retire or take a different job, you'll still want to be developing others who can fill your shoes if the need arises.

You'll want to invest in developing, sponsoring, shaping, and helping release someone else toward greater ministry potential. The role God calls them to may be in a different ministry from your own, or they may take *your* role someday.

A few years ago I had the honor of participating in a succession ceremony. The influential founding pastor of a large Sacramento church was stepping down from the senior pastor role to pursue a new ministry role he felt God calling him to. Over the previous few years he'd been intentionally developing a young man in his church to take on the role of leading the church forward into the next generation.

I've seldom seen such a moving service. I thought of the image of a long-distance race where one runner hands off the baton to the next runner, and in the ceremony they actually passed on a baton with some writing on it to the new pastor as a symbol. I think the practice originated with the passing of the Olympic torch. But we do the same thing in ministry, don't we? It's a long-distance run, not a sprint. No matter how important you are, your days in ministry will end and someone else's will begin.

Moses passed the baton to Joshua. What made that handoff so successful? Moses prepared Joshua beforehand, he prepared the people beforehand, and he willingly allowed Joshua to begin making decisions. Moses also gave young Joshua powerful words of blessing and encouragement: "Be strong and courageous. Do not be afraid or terrified because of them, for the Lord your God goes with you; he will never leave you nor forsake you" (Deut. 31:6).

So pass the baton to a new generation of leaders. Passing the baton is not a symbol of failure, but of success. It does not mean that you are "done"; it just frees you up for what God has for you next—and it prepares for the church to go on, even when you are no longer there to guide it yourself.

Consider who God might be calling you to invest in and develop. Who is open? What do they need? What do you have to offer? Consider what skills and behaviors you can help them develop. Consider how you can sponsor them into your ministry organization. We never know what God might do, but we do know it will go beyond each of us individually.

Look to the road ahead

Set your ministry up for success. Shift gears to avoid stalling out, so you can continue on the road ahead. Things you do now—even if you are early on in your ministry role—can make a significant difference later.

> We never know what God might do, but we do know it will go beyond each of us individually.

The first time I planted a church back in the late 1970s, I knew another guy who was also planting. He was an extremely gifted evangelist. He would go door to door, and it seemed like people were just waiting to ask him what they must do to be saved. His evangelistic growth was phenomenal in the early stages, and a good many new believers became a part of his church. But after a while, that growth plateaued—because he limited himself to what he personally did.

I was not—and am not—similarly gifted. But when the balance shifted from what I could do to what I could equip others to do, our growth took off. Even more importantly, that growth was sustainable, as more and more people became effective in relational evangelism reaching their own networks. The church grew steadily and, in the long run, had a far greater evangelistic impact.

Prayer guide

- Who is currently serving as a coach or guide to you? Who could be?

- How do you take time for listening prayer and planning for the future?

- What transitions are necessary for the next stage of ministry? For you personally? For your organization?

- Who is God laying on your heart to develop and invest in?

- What next steps are you sensing God might have you take now?

For further reading:

- *Finding the Flow: A guide for leading small groups and gatherings,* by Tara Miller and Jenn Peppers

- *Reframing Organizations: Artistry, Choice, and Leadership*, by Lee G. Bolman and Terrence E. Deal

- *The Essential Drucker: The Best of Sixty Years of Peter Drucker's Essential Writings on Management*, by Peter F. Drucker

12

FINANCIAL AND LEGAL PRACTICALITIES

Staying Out of Jail

I once consulted with a pastor who told me, "We're within budget, but we're broke." He had been faithfully and meticulously tracking everything and staying within budget each month, but then suddenly found himself unable to pay the bills. The problem? The budget was annual, but the bills were primarily monthly, with some staggered expenses. For instance, the church may have an insurance payment due in April, but the church can't pay it all then if not all the funds have come in yet. You need to have enough in the budget *and* in the bank. It's like a personal or family budget. You may have a certain amount to spend per year, but if your son needs his wisdom teeth out in July, you'll need to plan in advance for that expense.

There are a lot of different ways to get off track financially in the church, and you have to watch them all at once. It's like a driver saying, "I was so focused on going the speed limit that I went into the ditch." You have to go the speed limit, stay centered in your lane, pay attention to the stopping distance between you and the car in front of you, and remember to have turned on the headlights beforehand. There are multiple tasks at once.

In fact, misuse of funds—in all of its infinite variety—is one the easiest and fastest ways to destroy a church. It could be a church, a denomination, a compassion ministry, a missions organization—any kind of organization that handles money. That includes both intentional and unintentional misuse. Being responsible with church funds is essential for both the health of the ministry and the reputation of the church worldwide.

> Misuse of church funds—in all of its infinite variety—is one the easiest and fastest ways to destroy a church.

That has been true since the earliest days of the church. Consider how Paul prepared the offering from the Corinthian church to the Macedonian church and sent it along, ensuring that it would arrive safely. The principle was "generous, yet wise,"—a good guiding principle for all of us in ministry as well.

Our desire is not that others might be relieved while you are hard pressed, but that there might be equality. At the present time your plenty will supply what they need, so that in turn their plenty will supply what you need. The goal is equality, as it is written: "The one who gathered much did not have too much, and the one who gathered little did not have too little."

Thanks be to God, who put into the heart of Titus the same concern I have for you. For Titus not only welcomed our appeal, but he is coming to you with much enthusiasm and on his own initiative. And we are sending along with him the brother who is praised by all the churches for his service to the gospel. What is more, he was chosen by the churches to accompany us as we carry the offering, which we administer in order to honor the Lord himself and to show our eagerness to help. We want to avoid any criticism of the way we administer this liberal gift. For we are taking pains to do what is right, not only in the eyes of the Lord but also in the eyes of man (2 Cor. 8:13–21).

The apostle Paul's goal was to manage the gift well—"to honor the Lord," "to show our eagerness to help," "to avoid any criticism," and to take "pains to do what is right, not only in the eyes of the Lord but also in the eyes of man." Notice that one piece of the plan was to have Titus accompany them with the gift, so no one could be accused of tampering with it. Generous, yet wise. They wanted to handle the money well, and went to some trouble to do so. That is our goal as well.

This chapter is about the very practical matter of handling money well and legally for ministry organizations. We'll go over some best practices, as well as the underlying principles for handing ministry money well. Many pastors have little to no experience with running the financial side of a church. Odds are, you were not trained at seminary to run an organization with a budget— including income, expenses, and payroll. You probably took no business or accounting classes. Yet it's an essential part of church leadership.

Topics we'll cover in this chapter include:

- Character and integrity
- Transparency and safeguards
- Cash flow
- Connecting budgets to goals
- Congregation-wide communication and stewardship

Character and integrity

As leaders, we are responsible for administering the church's finances appropriately. Whether our ministry has a million-dollar budget or a small offering from ten people, we are still called to steward this money responsibly and use it in the manner for which it was intended. This means being honest, transparent, and making all decisions in line with kingdom values.

We need to live as though we are not permanent residents of this world—because we are not. We are entrusted with what we have for a time.

Motives are always important to examine when it comes to money as well. We need to be generous yet wise. We need to avoid greed and self-aggrandizement. We need to live as though we are not permanent residents of this world—because we are not. We are entrusted with what we have for a time, and God knows whether we are investing it well or poorly. That is especially true of ministry leaders. Paul writes to Timothy, urging that leaders and teachers avoid greed:

> These are the things you are to teach and insist on. If anyone teaches otherwise and does not agree to the sound instruction of our Lord Jesus Christ and to godly teaching, they are conceited and understand nothing. They have an unhealthy interest in controversies and quarrels about words that result in envy, strife, malicious talk, evil suspicions and constant friction between people of corrupt mind, who have been robbed of the truth and who think that godliness is a means to financial gain.
>
> But godliness with contentment is great gain. For we brought nothing into the world, and we can take nothing out of it. But if we have food and clothing, we will be content with that. Those who want to get rich fall into temptation and a trap and into many foolish and harmful desires that plunge people into ruin and destruction. For the love of money is a root of all kinds of evil. Some people, eager for money, have wandered from the faith and pierced themselves with many griefs.
>
> But you, man of God, flee from all this, and pursue righteousness, godliness, faith, love, endurance and gentleness. Fight the good fight of the faith. Take hold of the

eternal life to which you were called when you made your good confession in the presence of many witnesses. In the sight of God, who gives life to everything, and of Christ Jesus, who while testifying before Pontius Pilate made the good confession, I charge you to keep this command without spot or blame until the appearing of our Lord Jesus Christ, which God will bring about in his own time—God, the blessed and only Ruler, the King of kings and Lord of lords, who alone is immortal and who lives in unapproachable light, whom no one has seen or can see. To him be honor and might forever. Amen.

Command those who are rich in this present world not to be arrogant nor to put their hope in wealth, which is so uncertain, but to put their hope in God, who richly provides us with everything for our enjoyment. Command them to do good, to be rich in good deeds, and to be generous and willing to share. In this way they will lay up treasure for themselves as a firm foundation for the coming age, so that they may take hold of the life that is truly life.

Timothy, guard what has been entrusted to your care. Turn away from godless chatter and the opposing ideas of what is falsely called knowledge, which some have professed and in so doing have departed from the faith (1 Tim. 6:2–21).

This passage, written specifically to church leaders about money, packs in a lot. Read back over it slowly, underlining phrases that particularly stand out to you. What changes might God want to make in your heart regarding the ways you manage ministry money?

Transparency and safeguards

The passage from 2 Corinthians we looked at earlier in this chapter illustrates the concepts of transparency and safeguarding. Paul told people about the offering beforehand, and involved multiple people getting it where it was intended to go, so no one person had charge of the money alone at any given time.

Likewise, we need clear, transparent, and safe ways to handle money in our ministries. These should be ways that not only keep the money safe, but also keep us safe from any potential accusations of wrongdoing. Putting some guidelines in place can be a vital safeguard for yourself and your ministry. Here are a few I recommend:

Accounting: Create a clear and transparent system for monitoring and tracking the money. An accountant or someone with basic accounting skills can record income and expenses, and compare that to the budget. A clear paper trail of everything is essential. Remember that the words "accounting" and "accountability" have the same root for a reason.

Safeguarding: Safeguarding includes practices like keeping receipts, and making sure the same person doesn't do the books and sign the checks. It's creating a system of checks and balances that protects your church against any accusations or misuse of money.

More than one person: One of the most important things is to have multiple people involved with the church finances. If one person has too much control over the money, the temptation can be great. Don't put any of your leaders, including yourself, in that position. When the offering is collected, have more than one person involved.

Establish your church or ministry as a legal entity: Register as a nonprofit organization according to the laws in your country. Then make sure your systems and practices are in line with all legal requirements. This process usually involves annual filing at tax-time even for tax-exempt organizations. It's worth hiring someone at the very beginning to ensure full compliance.

> **Remember that the words "accounting" and "accountability" have the same root for a reason.**

Cash flow

Cash Flow Management

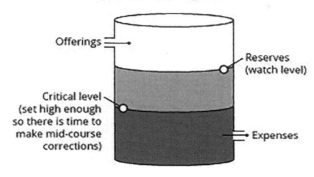

When I coach leaders in the area of their finances, I like to use the image of a water tank. Water comes in at the top and out at the bottom. The water level in the tank signifies cash in the bank. Positive cash flow means that the water level is rising: There is more coming in than going out. Negative cash flow means the water level is falling: More water is leaving than is coming in.

When we are having challenges, we need to figure out to how to either decrease expenses or increase income. (It's also a good idea to see if you have any leaks and, if so, patch them.) We must either decrease the water going out or increase the water coming in, or the tank will run dry.

One good strategy is to identify when to set an alarm. When the tank gets to a certain low level, a cautionary alarm should go off—for example, when you only have two or three months' money in reserve. An alarm should go off at that point, indicating that action is needed—cut back on unnecessary expenses.

If the level continues to go down, then a second serious alarm should go off when the tank is nearly empty (one month's reserve). This is crisis mode. When you're in crisis mode, you need to embrace extreme measures. *You can only spend this month what came in the previous month.*

As long as you only spend next month what came in last month, you'll never go broke. As long as you are taking in more than you are spending, you'll always have reserves.

Be aware also of when big bills are due. Not all bills are due monthly. Even if you know you will have more money coming in soon, it needs to be there before you can spend it. If you have a large insurance payment due in April, you'll need to plan for that in advance. Weigh carefully the timing of major expenditures, and make sure you have enough in the account ahead of time to cover them—otherwise you can technically be within budget, but still broke, as we saw in the opening story for this chapter. It's not just a matter of staying within budget, but paying attention to cash flow as well so you can keep your expenses in pace with your incoming resources.

Connecting budgets to goals

But what about budgets? That's also an important item to consider. Most church leaders have a general sense of budgets just based on household examples, e.g., "We have X amount for rent, Y amount for food, and Z amount for insurance." As anyone who has run a household knows, setting and sticking to a budget is essential for long-term financial health.

Yet there's another side to budgets that we often don't think about: tying budgets to goals. How do you make sure your money is going to the most important parts of your ministry that will truly help propel the whole organization forward? If you value outreach and have set your ministry goals around reaching the surrounding community, but you are spending ninety percent of your budget internally, that's a budget/goal mismatch. Just like it is with people, if we look at how ministry organizations spend their money, we can see what is truly valued.

A note from Colin:

Bob is touching on a really important point here. When I start a coaching relationship with a new leader/pastor, I spend time asking questions that give me some idea of the values, mission, and vision of the organisation/church. I then ask for a copy of how they spend money. It is not hard to see if the beliefs of the church are ill-defined and fluffy, or are sharp and focused.

Don't start by setting a budget. First, figure out what you're trying to accomplish, then what that will cost. Put all the proposals together (from various staff people, if you have more than one area of ministry), and as a team prioritize what's most important to the overall mission right now.

> Just like it is with people, if we look at how ministry organizations spend their money, we can see what is truly valued.

Then consider the worth of the goals themselves. Is the amount of investment (time, money, personnel) worth the potential return? Don't just give money to staff members to put into their ministry. Have a clear goal for what they are supposed to accomplish with it. No goals equals no budget. Each staff person or ministry leader must be clear about what goals they're supposed to accomplish with the funding they have.

It's worth taking the time and energy to think through how to spend your resources wisely, so that they align with what you're trying to accomplish. The end result will be much stronger than simply trying to make rent and payroll each month. Money needs to be spent on mission, and God will hold us accountable for how we steward the money he has placed under our care.

Having a budget tied to your goals is the place to start. Expenditures should equal accomplished goals for the ministry. Yet be sure not to be too short-term focused; you'll also need to look forward into the future. Sometimes the things we need to invest in may not be those that bear immediate fruit, but that bear longer-term fruit.

What is truly important in the kingdom of God? That is what we should invest in. We also need to invest appropriately. What types of spending will yield fruit and get the long-term results we are looking for?

We don't need bean *counters*—we need bean *growers*. We need to focus on increasing capacity. By investing in what's working we can continue expanding the work of the ministry. For example, if you hire the right staff people—those who develop others—they will help you reach and serve more people, in turn generating increased cash flow to hire additional staff who will reach others... and so on. At the senior-leader level, we always need to be looking for those who develop others and increase overall ministry capacity. That's an investment that inevitably pays for itself.

Congregation-wide communication and stewardship

In addition to doing all the right things financially with your organization, you also need to be telling people about it. Establish regular, transparent communication with your whole congregation about how the money is being handled. Often email or newsletters can be a good way to go about keeping everyone informed. Congregational meetings (with take-home handouts) can also be helpful. The principle here is to tell people periodically—whether they have asked or not—how the money is being used. Simply communicating regularly, whether people pay much attention or not, increases the sense of trust and transparency.

> The principle here is to tell people periodically—whether they have asked or not—how the money is being used.

Be up front about how much money is coming in, when, and how. Then be up front about expenses and what that money is being used for. If you consistently donate ten percent of your income to world missions, people should know that. If you are contributing a certain amount toward a longer-term building fund or training initiative, people should know about that, too. In this way, everyone in your congregation should be able to see your organizational values reflected in your budget numbers.

Budget check

> When Paul and Barnabas were sent out to minister to the Gentiles, the other apostles had only one requirement: "All they asked was that we should continue to remember the poor, the very thing I had been eager to do all along" (Gal. 2:10). How does your church budget reflect that same priority?

Make financial information clear and readily accessible. This doesn't necessarily mean divulging individual salaries, but providing overall amounts of staffing, giving, facilities, etc. It also means being clear about the giving side of things, too. If offerings are down, that should be communicated. That way, when you need to make tough decisions to cut spending, everyone knows why it needed to be done.

Part of using church funds well is encouraging people to participate in the financial life of the church through giving. They are called to steward well what they have by using their personal money appropriately, saving, and giving generously. We can help people do that by teaching about stewardship and helping them to budget.

Talking about money should be kingdom-based. There are more Scriptures in the New Testament about money than anything else other than the kingdom of God. Good organisational stewardship can encourage people to explore the alignment between their attitude to money and their spiritual life.

God has an interesting goal: not just to change our behaviour to align with what He wants, but to bring our minds and hearts into alignment with Him as well. Believe it or not, this means even our money. When you think about money and your spiritual life, what connections come to mind? How easy is it for you to imagine your spiritual life extending into your wallet?

Generosity often requires some preparation:

There is no need for me to write to you about this service to the Lord's people. For I know your eagerness to help, and I have been boasting about it to the Macedonians, telling them that since last year you in Achaia were ready to give; and your enthusiasm has stirred most of them to action. But I am sending the brothers in order that our boasting about you in this matter should not prove hollow, but that you may be ready, as I said you would be. For if any Macedonians come with me and find you unprepared, we—not to say anything about you—would be ashamed of having been so confident. So I thought it necessary to urge the brothers to visit you in advance and finish the arrangements for the generous gift you had promised. Then it will be ready as a generous gift, not as one grudgingly given (2 Cor. 9:1–5).

Creating transparent systems so everyone is a part of the giving, and so everyone knows how the offerings are being used, will involve some advance planning. However, it is essential for faithful

FINANCIAL AND LEGAL PRACTICALITIES

stewardship of the resources God has given us. In all things—
including money—we are to be above reproach:

> Here is a trustworthy saying: "Whoever aspires to be an
> overseer desires a noble task. Now the overseer is to
> be above reproach, faithful to his wife, temperate, self-
> controlled, respectable, hospitable, able to teach, not given to
> drunkenness, not violent but gentle, not quarrelsome, not a
> lover of money" (1 Tim. 2:1–3).

Prayer guide

- To what degree does your ministry budget reflect kingdom values? What needs to be adjusted?

- How can you encourage those you lead to handle their money both wisely and generously? How are you leading by example?

- How are you communicating transparently with your congregation? How could that be improved?

- As you look through the systems described, where are you doing well? What is missing or needs improvement?

- What action steps are you sensing God would have you take in this area?

For further reading:

- *Money Matters in Church: A Practical Guide for Leaders*, by Aubrey Malphurs and Steve Stroope

13

EMPOWERING AND RELEASING OTHERS

Giving It All Away

There was once a small Hispanic church in New York City. The same pastor led the church for more than twenty years, as they planted church after church after church out of it. The original church never grew beyond its original small size; they just kept giving away people and money and people and money, planting something like twenty-seven new churches out of it. Finally, the church had given so much that it wasn't able to sustain itself. The pastor got old and tired, and the church had to close its doors.

They held a memorial service for the ministry of the church. As the pastor sat in the front row, hundreds of people came forward, one by one, all day long, to give testimony of how God had changed their lives and how they were helped—how thousands were reached, and thousands more ministered to and served—all by the generosity ministry of this one small church. The old pastor was weeping tears of joy as he saw the fruit of his life's work in a scope beyond what he ever expected.

I imagine that when we come before the throne in hopes of hearing, "Well done, good and faithful servant," this man will be near the head of the line. The greatest of the rewards in heaven may go to some people we've never heard of because they practiced kingdom values.

> Very truly I tell you, unless a kernel of wheat falls to the ground and dies, it remains only a single seed. But if it dies, it produces many seeds. Anyone who loves their life will lose it, while anyone who hates their life in this world will keep it for eternal life (John 12:24–25).

If you give your life away, you will surely find it. God calls us to selflessly give and give, but consider how much other life multiplies and lives into today because of that generosity. We sow seeds, most of the time never knowing where they will land or how they will grow. But God multiplies the impulses of our hears—sometimes thirty, sixty, a hundred times what was sown.

> He taught them many things by parables, and in his teaching said: "Listen! A farmer went out to sow his seed. As he was scattering the seed, some fell along the path, and the birds came and ate it up. Some fell on rocky places, where it did not have much soil. It sprang up quickly, because the soil was shallow. But when the sun came up, the plants were scorched, and they withered because they had no root. Other seed fell among thorns, which grew up and choked the plants, so that they did not bear grain. Still other seed fell on good soil. It came up, grew and produced a crop, some multiplying thirty, some sixty, some a hundred times." Then Jesus said, "Whoever has ears to hear, let them hear" (Mark 4:2–9).

Real leadership—biblical leadership—is about giving away ministry responsibility and decision-making authority, not keeping it for yourself. It's about equipping others to do what you do. Biblical leadership means passing the baton rather that keeping it for oneself or even one's own organization. We need to hold all that we have accomplished and developed with open hands, knowing it's not our own. It's God's to do with as he wishes.

> **Real leadership—biblical leadership—is about giving away ministry responsibility and decision-making authority, not keeping it for yourself. It's about equipping others to do what you do.**

The final chapter of this book brings us full circle. It's about releasing new leaders and new organizations, empowering them and sending them out to continue the work of the ministry.

Topics we'll cover include:

- Servant leadership

- Developing others for mission

- Fostering kingdom cooperation

- Releasing and empowering well

Servant leadership

Biblical leadership begins with a radical posture of humility. Consider how Jesus came to us—as an infant, in human flesh, he was at his most defenseless. Jesus entered an insecure situation, where his parents were poor and traveling in an unfamiliar land. He entered a fallen world—one where a powerful king was hunting for him, in order to kill him. He had no resources, advocates, or worldly power. He embodied human frailty in all its vulnerability.

Because of this, Jesus understands our own vulnerability on an intimate level. He knows that even as we who are Christian leaders try to shepherd others, we have our own weaknesses and difficulties, our own wounds and temptations. He understands that reality, and we need to embrace its truth for ourselves as well.

Just as you personally don't have it all together, neither does your church or ministry. It's easy to point fingers at other groups and say, "We're better than them." Don't fall into that trap. You may have different issues, but you can still learn from one another. Don't consider yourselves better than others. Humility is the first step toward true leadership.

> Then the mother of Zebedee's sons came to Jesus with her sons and, kneeling down, asked a favor of him.
>
> "What is it you want?" he asked.
>
> She said, "Grant that one of these two sons of mine may sit at your right and the other at your left in your kingdom."
>
> "You don't know what you are asking," Jesus said to them. "Can you drink the cup I am going to drink?"
>
> "We can," they answered.
>
> Jesus said to them, "You will indeed drink from my cup, but to sit at my right or left is not for me to grant. These places belong to those for whom they have been prepared by my Father." When the ten heard about this, they were indignant with the two brothers. Jesus called them together and said, "You know that the rulers of the Gentiles lord it over them, and their high officials exercise authority over them. Not so with you. Instead, whoever wants to become great among you must be your servant, and whoever wants to be first must be your slave—just as the Son of Man did not come to be served, but to serve, and to give his life as a ransom for many" (Matt. 20:20–28).

Lots of people want to become leaders. And certainly, leaders are necessary, but the real key is attitude: humility and openness to serving outside of the spotlight. To continue growing and changing to become more and more Christlike as servant leaders, we need to move forward in a spirit of humility. Humility is what leaves us open to change and to God's correction in our lives. Set aside

ROBERT E. LOGAN | LOGANLEADERSHIP.COM

some time to reflect on your life in a spirit of humility. Where are you open to change? Where are you not?

> **A note from Colin:**
>
> In 1970 Robert K. Greenleaf published a classic essay, "The Servant as Leader." Greenleaf wrote 'The servant-leader is servant first.... It begins with the natural feeling that one wants to serve, to serve first. Then conscious choice brings one to aspire to lead. That person is sharply different from one who is leader first. The difference manifests itself in the care taken by the servant—first to make sure that other people's highest priority needs are being served. The best test, and difficult to administer, is: Do those served grow as persons? Do they, while being served, become healthier, wiser, freer, more autonomous, more likely themselves to become servants?" This definition puts Christian leadership in perspective.

Then consider the outward focus of humility: How are we to live out a radically generous life? How are we to live wisely, stewarding well what God has given us? Into what additional areas of our lives can generosity extend?

> **To continue growing and changing to become more and more Christlike as servant leaders, we need to move forward in a spirit of humility.**

Developing others for mission

Part of that generosity and humility is in developing others for the purpose of mission. Many senior leaders are eager to raise up more leaders to work beneath them within their own organization. But how many are willing to invest in raising up more leaders to send them out to other ministries? How many are willing to raise up others who will take their own place?

It's the ultimate case of working yourself out of a job, yet it does need to be considered. Succession is most often done by accident, at the time it becomes an obvious need: an unexpected death, retirement, job change, or moral failing. Those times are difficult enough in and of themselves without also having to begin thinking about a succession plan—and getting it done yesterday.

Yet if you have been intentional about raising up others who can take your place, you're well positioned for such a transition. Many churches and other ministries fall apart or decline at these critical points, but if you plan for your succession in advance you can mitigate much of the potential damage and even make it a redemptive and positive experience for all involved. The critical point: Plan for your succession before you know you need to. No matter what your role, someone else needs to be able to replace you.

Of course, this requires humility and trust in God to really embrace and implement. Yet it's not just what you do during your tenure as senior leader but also how you leave matters for the next generation of the church that really makes for a lasting legacy. Succession is not an "if" but a "when." The question is how you will handle it.

By being intentional, proactive, and outward-focused, you can develop other leaders for mission who can do what you do— either in your ministry environment or in others. You never know where the people you send off on mission will end up. Like passing the Olympic torch to the next runner, you hope it's further than you can get yourself.

> For whoever wants to save their life will lose it, but whoever loses their life for me will find it (Matt. 16:25).

Fostering kingdom cooperation

Sometimes we think of local churches as if they were restaurants. They compete with one another for market share. Eating at one place means you are not eating at the other place. Therefore, you have a vested interest in offering better food and service than the other restaurants, so that you can cut into their business.

Not so with the church—at least that's not how God intended it. There are more than enough people who need God to go around. Different churches, far from competing with one another, have a vested interest in helping and strengthening one another. The stronger each local church becomes, the stronger the whole church universal becomes.

The same is true of nonprofit organizations and other ministries. Why start your own food pantry when you can partner with one that already exists? Less overhead and administration, and more people get served.

There's no place for competition between churches and leaders in the kingdom of God. We are called to serve and to be last, not first. That means not only developing and releasing other new leaders into ministry, but also giving and helping other organizations.

Consider the community around you. Who is already at work there? Are there churches already present? Even if they are from different backgrounds, you can cooperate with one another. What other ministries, small groups, and/or leaders are there? You're probably not the first on the scene.

Given who is already there and the work they have been doing, how can you be of help? Maybe they have been praying for a certain resource or gift—and you are God's answer. How can you bless what they are doing, even if it's not of direct benefit to your organization?

As you cooperate with other ministries in the area, there may be some you have a natural affinity with. What type of ongoing partnerships might be mutually beneficially for both the ministries and the community? Be willing to be a part of what God might have for you, even if it wasn't part of your own plan.

Releasing and empowering well

Ultimately, the church is not many—it's one. We aren't to compete against other churches and ministries for people or resources. We're on the same side. We can help and support one another, all of us becoming stronger in the process.

To do this well, we must be willing to give up control and release power to other people and organizations. That means not just delegating tasks, but delegating responsibility and decision-making ability. It means developing others who can lead, not just take orders. It means watching people to see when they are ready, and then letting them have incremental freedom to go out on their own. It means providing support and resources, but not micromanaging.

A note from Colin:

In their book The Pin Drop Principle, David Lewis and Riley Mills include a list of lousy leadership practices. They suggest that lousy leadership begins with self-protective attitudes—not lack of skills, intelligence, or talent. Lousy leaders:

- *Need to know more than others.*
- *Need their egos stroked.*
- *Fear high performers; they need the spotlight.*
- *Struggle to collaborate.*
- *Won't change their minds.*
- *Feel isolated and alone.*
- *Sacrifice long-term success for short-term results*

Releasing power well is in the blood of great leaders. As you review and consider what Bob has written in this book, ask yourself: "What sort of leader am I?" Remember, poor leadership begins with self-protective attitudes—not lack of skills, intelligence, or talent.

All of this is easier said than done, and needs to be calculated within the context of relationship and conversation to see when and in what ways new leaders are ready to move out on their own. Like a kid leaving home for the first time, some safety features and check-ins may be in place, but there's also a lot of new freedom. That freedom is incremental, but it needs to be moving in the *direction* of freedom. That likely means making mistakes, but that's an inevitable part of letting go and allowing people to mature into all that God has for them.

As you release power to new leaders, consider the following:

- What decision-making powers are you giving up?
- What support are you still providing?
- What check-in conversations will still be in place?
- How will you ensure that you can step back enough to let them make their own decisions?
- What support do they still need?
- How will the relationship look different in a month? In six months? In a year?

Without releasing and empowering well, Paul would never have developed Timothy, and the ministry of the church would grind to a halt in one generation. We need to release new leaders in order to keep going forward:

> And the things you have heard me say in the presence of many witnesses entrust to reliable people who will also be qualified to teach others (2 Tim. 2:2).

The church in Honduras has what they call "extension chains," based on 2 Timothy 2:2. An extension chain is essential a series of people who have heard the gospel and passed it on to trustworthy people, who then continue to pass it on. When I was there attending a training workshop, they called up six men and lined them up into an extension chain. The one on the far left had introduced the man on his right to the gospel and started a church. That man in turn had introduced the man on his right to the gospel and also started a church, and so on. The church leadership was able to pull these people up from the crowd, just out of who happened to be there that day.

Additionally, raising up new followers of Jesus is seen there culturally as closely connected to church planting. People are won to Christ and raised up as leaders, who then pastor churches. That leader is expected to continue the multiplication by winning other people and raising up other leaders, who will then go on to plant more churches.

Each person in the extension chain I saw that day was raised up as a convert, and developed into a pastoral leader and church multiplier. Each of those men represented a church that had been started. It was one of the most powerful pictures I have ever seen of empowerment and passing it on. We must all—wherever God has placed us—multiply and give away leadership if we are to play our part in contributing to the vision of the kingdom of God.

> *After this I looked, and there before me was a great multitude that no one could count, from every nation, tribe, people and language, standing before the throne and before the Lamb. They were wearing white robes and were holding palm branches in their hands. And they cried out in a loud voice: "Salvation belongs to our God, who sits on the throne, and to the Lamb" (Rev. 7:9–10).*

Prayer guide

- Who are you currently developing as a leader?

- What would it cost you to empower and release them to whatever God has for them?

- What other churches, ministries, or nonprofits do you have relationships with?

- In what ways might you be able to help them, even if they are not in a position to help you in return?

- What fears surround letting go of control?

- What do you need to repent of?

- What action steps are you sensing God would have you take?

For further reading:

- *Leadership Engine: How Winning Companies Build Leaders at Every Level*, by Noel M. Tichy

- *Baton Change: Releasing the Next Generation,* by Peter Lyne and John Dawson

- *The Leadership Pipeline: How to Build the Leadership Powered Company*, by Ram Charan, Stephen Drotter and James Noel

APPENDICES

DIMENSIONS OF DISCIPLESHIP

Experiencing God: Intentionally and consistently engaging with God in such a way that you open yourself to a deeper understanding of him and deeper relationship with him

Behavioral Expressions:

- Increasing your awareness of God's love and presence
- Growing in the knowledge and grace of God
- Reflecting on and applying scripture in your everyday life
- Dialoguing authentically with God
- Worshipping God in spirit and in truth

Spiritual Responsiveness: Actively listening to the Holy Spirit, and taking action according to what you are hearing

Behavioral Expressions:

- Receiving guidance and empowerment from the Holy Spirit
- Discerning opportunities for involvement in God's work
- Checking what you're hearing with Scripture and your faith community
- Acting in faith through loving obedience
- Listening for God's calling in your life

Sacrificial Service: Doing good works even when it's costly, inconvenient, or challenging

Behavioral Expressions:

- Blessing others with your words and deeds
- Partnering with others to minister in practical ways
- Ministering personally and appropriately to the poor
- Speaking up for people experiencing injustice
- Cultivating a compassionate heart

Disciplemaking: Living in obedience to the great commission given by Jesus, which entails making more and better followers of Christ

Behavioral Expressions:

- Engaging in spiritual conversations with those who are not yet followers of Jesus

- Explaining the good news and the way of Jesus

- Establishing new believers in a discipleship process

- Connecting people with a faith community

- Helping new followers make more followers

Personal Transformation: Changing your attitudes and behaviors in positive ways as a result of your relationship with God and others

Behavioral Expressions:

- Actively engaging with God in the examination of your heart

- Cooperating with God's healing work in your life

- Processing feedback and input from others

- Living out new priorities and changed behavior

- Increasingly bearing the fruit of the Spirit

Authentic Relationships: Engaging with other people in ways that reflect the heart of God toward them

Behavioral Expressions:

- Showing respect for all people

- Forgiving others and asking forgiveness

- Confronting others with humility as necessary

- Praying with and for others

- Supporting each other honestly through life challenges

Community Transformation: Personal involvement with others to facilitate positive change, where you live and beyond

Behavioral Expressions:

- Participating in a faith community that reaches outside of itself

- Praying for healing and reconciliation in society

- Involving yourself in social justice needs in the broader community

- Caring for God's creation in practical ways

- Helping others cultivate healthy lives and relationships

Generous Living: Faithfully stewarding what God has given you so you can contribute toward the advancement of the kingdom

Behavioral Expressions:

- Managing your time and resources for kingdom purposes

- Using your spiritual gifts to bless others

- Giving your money generously and wisely

- Showing hospitality without favoritism

- Living out your God-given calling

The dimensions of discipleship form the foundation for several resources available on our website and on Amazon.com. Read on for more information and links to more information.

LEADERSHIP SKILLS

Below is a list of competencies I put together, with the help of Dr. Chuck Ridley and Tara Miller. These are the skills we believe a growing disciple needs to possess in order to also be an effective leader.

Personal Development

- Continuing in spiritual formation
- Managing time
- Managing money
- Engaging in lifelong learning
- Focusing personal ministry contribution

Developing Leaders

- Identifying potential leaders
- Providing ministry opportunities
- Identifying giftedness and passion
- Training new leaders
- Providing ongoing challenges
- Providing ongoing support

Leading Teams

- Building community
- Leading meetings
- Facilitating learning
- Delegating
- Supervising leaders
- Coaching leaders
- Ministry and money

Organizational Development

- Clarifying values, mission, and vision
- Vision-casting
- Gaining ownership
- Prioritizing
- Goal-setting
- Planning
- Modifying
- Celebrating

Communication Skills

- Listening
- Asking questions
- Providing feedback
- Speaking the truth in love
- Resolving conflict
- Seeing through another's eyes

Pastoral Skills

- Shepherding

- Mentoring

- Public speaking

- Facilitating small groups

- Fostering kingdom cooperation

These 37 Leadership Skills form the foundation for the Leadership Skills Guides, available on our website.

ABOUT THE AUTHOR

Dr. Robert E. Logan has over 40 years of ministry experience, including church planting, pastoring, consulting, coaching, and speaking. Having seen a great deal, Bob remains on the cutting edge of ministry through hands-on missional involvement. Bob earned his DMin from Fuller Theological Seminary. He counts it a privilege to walk alongside ministry leaders and help catalyze their ministries toward fulfilling the call God has placed on them, and he thrives in developing holistic and transformative resources that can easily be implemented in any context. Bob enjoys cycling and volunteering in a recovery community.

ABOUT LOGAN LEADERSHIP

Our vision is every person living, growing and multiplying together as disciples of Jesus who demonstrate the Kingdom of God among all peoples.

Our mission is catalyzing leaders to accelerate their movement toward this vision.

Our approach integrates biblical principles with social science insights by helping leaders...

- sharpen thinking skills

- focus actions

- contextualize solutions

- create reproducible processes

- increase ministry capacity

Find out more about us at http://loganleadership.com.

LOVE GOD|LOVE OTHERS|MAKE DISCIPLES

Logan Leadership is the central hub for information and resources to assist you in your personal growth and your ministry. With decades of experience coaching and consulting with leaders worldwide, our desire is to equip leaders to live, grow, and multiply together as disciples of Jesus who demonstrate the Kingdom of God among all peoples.

We're all about helping you get where you want to go. That looks different for each ministry or organization. Depending on your goals, we can provide targeted coaching, training, resource development, assessment, and/or consulting.

Over the years, we've helped hundreds of churches, denominations and mission organizations meet and exceed their goals. That can mean implementing discipleship processes, retooling leadership development, turning around congregations in decline, or any number of other aims.

Coaching — The accountability and clarity that coaching provides gives you the follow through you need to accomplish the goals you've set for yourself and your ministry.

Consulting — We can enter your ministry situation to help you find contextualized solutions for your specific needs.

Training — We design interactive training systems geared toward coaches, church planters, disciplers, pastors and key leaders.

Resource Development — We can create and/or adapt Logan Leadership resources that speak effectively and appropriately to the culture and people of your organization.

Assessments — Using God's Word and proven social science insights, we offer a number of effective assessment tools that help you and your organization make smart decisions.

Find out more at https://loganleadership.com.

DISCIPLESHIP RESOURCES

To fulfill the Great Commission, we must be faithful to make disciples of Jesus. Logan Leadership has created several resources to assist you in your personal discipleship journey and in encouraging others toward a closer walk with God.

The Discipleship Difference — Every person is different and we all reflect God in different ways. So why is our typical approach to discipleship the same across the board? The Discipleship Difference lays out an intentional, holistic, and relational approach to discipleship that is individualized to meet each person wherever they are.

The Discipleship Difference is available in print and Kindle at http://amazon.com or at https://loganleadership.com/DD. Contact us for bulk discount.

Guide for Discipling — Logan Leadership created the Guide for Discipling to encourage disciples new and old to love God, love others, and make disciples. With a total of forty lessons, each is supported by related scriptures and includes thought-provoking questions to encourage discussion. Pastors, church leaders, and individuals can use these guides in a variety of ways to grow in holistic discipleship.

We have also collaborated with several denominations to offer versions of the Guide for Discipling which relate in a way that is most appropriate for that denomination. Visit the Discipleship Guides Shop to learn more and to purchase your copy at: https://loganleadership.com/G4D. Also available in print and Kindle at http://amazon.com.

Discipleship Cohort — How many years have you been trying to get discipleship going in your context? Are you willing to try something different? The Discipleship Cohort is a year-long cohort for implementing discipleship in your ministry context. Offered only once per year, this group is a deep dive into  the eight dimensions of discipleship outlined in the companion book for this course, The Discipleship Difference.

Check https://loganleadership.com/DC for details on the next open application period.

Disciple Assessment — Your church will only grow as well as the disciples that you develop. How can you reliably measure discipleship progress? The portrait of Jesus in the four gospels serves as our guide. Disciples seek to live and love like Jesus. The Disciple Assessment provides a  snapshot of where you are in 8 dimensions of a disciple of Jesus, and is appropriate for individuals, small groups, churches, and missional communities.

Learn more at http://discipleassessment.com.

LEADERSHIP RESOURCES

Leadership Skills Guides — This comprehensive set of Leadership Skills leader guides covers 37 essential leadership skills. Each guide includes a written introduction, teaching points, scripture passages and reflection, and discussion questions. Every topic has participant guides to hand out

to those you are training and leader guides for yourself that give you a bit more content. There's even a section that lays out various options for covering the material with those you're training. Learn more and purchase your copy at:

https://loganleadership.com/LSG.

TRAINING OPPORTUNITIES

As a ministry leader, you know how difficult it can be to gather a group together for training. What if you could gather together virtually to walk through training together?

Logan Leadership offers an online training specifically for pastors and ministry leaders who want to train others via Sublimeety, a subscription-based web platform that establishes flexible processes to facilitate more efficient and productive  virtual meetings and trainings. This training material is highly interactive and offers special resources and practical exercises to sharpen your team's group leadership skills. We give you the tools, and you add your unique perspective to personalize the experience for your leaders. Want to learn more? Visit us at: http://go-sublime.com.

ACKNOWLEDGMENTS

Foremost thanks for this book go to all those I've served alongside in ministry. The best learning is through experience, and you all have helped me become rich in that. I'm blessed to have journeyed alongside you and have learned much from you.

I am also grateful to Colin Noyes for his feedback and commentary on the manuscript, to Dr. Charles Ridley for his help framing the skills, to Carl Simmons for editing, to Douglas Williams for formatting, and to Marcy Bradford and Michelle Coe for endless hours spent shepherding this project to completion. Michelle also contributed the photograph for the cover of the book.

Much gratitude also goes to those who helped me select and narrow down my recommended reading for the end of each chapter. So much has been written that I would not be able to compile a helpful list without multiple perspectives from you all: Christian Lunde, Colin Noyes, Michael Gatlin, Christina Roberts, and Nick Warnes.

And special thanks go to Tara Miller, who has teamed with me in writing for many years. She is able to take my thoughts and weave them into words in ways that I could never do.

Finally, I'd like to acknowledge all of the future readers, whose leadership I pray will be more effective through the application of the principles found in this book.

Made in the USA
Columbia, SC
22 May 2018